CW00518219

Editorial

Welcome to TOTAL **PREDATOR** FISHING, which is dedicated to the predator angler old and new.

The beginning of the 21st century has seen predator fishing become cool! From early October until late spring, the banks of our rivers and stillwaters become a draw for pike and zander anglers enjoying some incredible sport fishing on baits and lures. Big perch are also high up the list of the specimen predator angler. These fish have flourished in commercial fisheries and rivers where, in the latter, they grow huge thanks to a diet of crayfish.

How times have changed! Over 30 years ago the coarse and game hierarchy saw pike as a nuisance predator feeding on their trout and salmon stocks, and much sought-after specimen roach. So much so that annual culling sessions would take place each winter on many sections of rivers throughout the British Isles. Then came all the brouhaha about the illegal stocking of zander and catfish into our waters.

Today, dedicated specimen hunters spend many hours on the bank in search of a big zander, as well as a 100lb catfish, of which there are a few.

To catch a big eel is not an easy task, as the species is on the decline in this country, but find the right location and that 5lb-plus fish is possible. Oh, and did you know that big chub love smashing into lures and small pieces of deadbait?

To catch these predators you need to fish the right baits, on the right rigs, and on many occasions put in a lot of time. You also need a lot of luck. However, the rewards can be well worth the effort.

Throughout Total Predator Fishing there are some inspirational features with top anglers, demonstrating just some of the many methods and baits you can fish. These include Mick Brown's kebab rig, Duncan Charman's eel adventures, a pike care feature and a cracking European lure piece.

There are also pages on the gear you need, together with sections on some popular rigs and how to make them, as well as answers to popular predator questions.

There are some big fish to be caught. The once-exclusive domain of the specimen carp angler – the gravel pit – can be home to pike in excess of 30lb. Some of our rivers now contain zander over the 20lb mark and perch to 6lb. And catfish? Well, if that's what takes your fancy, then there are plenty of venues to try your luck.

Whichever species you target I hope you enjoy reading Total Predator Fishing and it inspires you to get out on the bank, and get the adrenaline rush that only comes from a striking predator.

Steve Martin
Deputy Editor, Total Coarse Fishing

Contents
TOTAL PREDATOR FISHING

Perch on soft lures
page 36

TOTAL **PREDATOR** FISHING
Published by David Hall Publishing Ltd. The
advertisements and editorial content of this
publication are the copyright of David Hall
Publishing Ltd and may not be quoted, copied
or reproduced without prior permission of the
publisher.

Copyright © 2011
Edited by Steve Martin
Layout and design by Fiona Brett
Diagrams by Rebecca Abbott
Reprographics by Derek Mooney and Steph Horn
Sub edited by David Haynes

Monsters in the mist

Sleek, muscular and hard fighting. There's nothing to beat catching a big river pike in winter. **Steve Collett** knows just where to go for one…

I f you've never caught a fighting-fit river pike, then you don't know what you're missing! That's the clear message from Steve Collett as he carries his tackle down to the banks of the River Wye, in Hereford. Steve is a former Angling Trust Division One National Champion with 56kg of barbel from the River Trent… but he loves his pike fishing too!

The powerful Wye is regarded by many as the best running-water fishery in the country, home to some of the best natural-water pike sport anywhere in Britain during the winter months… and all for the price of a day ticket.

Why is the sport so good? "After October the lower reaches of the Wye become like an aquarium, with thousands of dace, chub and roach packing into the deeper water on the city reaches," says Steve.

"They probably feel relatively comfortable here and there is safety in numbers, but they must always live their lives in fear of predators… especially pike!"

Whenever fish are shoaled together in large numbers predators will be in attendance, and that has to be the first and most obvious lesson to be learnt when you intend to pursue pike on any kind of venue. Find the prey fish first, and the predators will rarely be too far away, awaiting their chance to pounce and eat their next meal.

Today there are small fish topping all over the river, clearly visible in the subdued light of dawn, and Steve is confident he is fishing in a good area.

"My main confidence comes from the expert

Steve Collett

Occupation: Retired
Hometown: Worcs
Sponsor: Harris
Sportsmail

Venue file

River Wye,
Belvedere Lane,
Hereford
Controlling club:
Hereford DAA
Day tickets: £6 in
advance from Woody's
Angling Centre, 67
Whitecross Road,
Hereford HR4 0DQ. Tel
01432 344644

**Winter fishing
doesn't get much
better than this.**

Steve's rig tips

01 Keep the tags long on the stop knot above the float to aid passage through the rod rings.

02 The Hardy & Greys Prowla 360 Paternoster Boom makes the rig very easy to create.

03 Use a ½oz to 2oz lead on a length of weaker line below the boom.

04 Hook the mackerel bait with the barbed hooks, leaving the barbless points clear.

local knowledge I have gleaned from tackle-shop owner Paul 'Woody' Woodward," he says. "There's nothing better than this kind of advice for swim selection. Locals know where the fish are from week to week and from year to year, as the cyclical movements of the fish are usually very predictable."

Steve's chosen swim is located below the footbridge at the end of Belvedere Lane in Hereford, in front of the rugby ground. This length holds plenty of silver fish in the winter months, and is reliable for pike too. "You still have to be lucky enough to tempt one, though!" says Steve.

It's a true 'piker's dawn' – the air is chilly and the residual, comparative warmth of the water in the river has created a thick veil of mist, which is hanging across the surrounding low-lying city of Hereford. It's an atmospheric vision, and strangely confidence-inspiring.

"The conditions certainly look the part; let's hope the pike are ready to feed too!" Steve declares, as he hurriedly sets up his rods, full of anticipation for the session ahead.

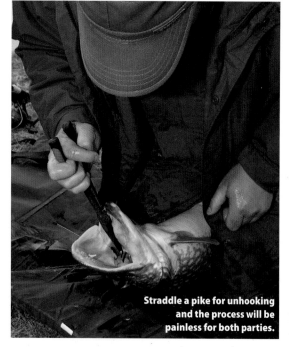
Straddle a pike for unhooking and the process will be painless for both parties.

The importance of river levels

As lovely as things look, what is even more important is the level of the river. Steve prefers to fish as the level is settling back down after being high. In a flood, the fish will have been forced to fight against the strong flow, which makes them use energy; they will need to eat as quickly as possible to replace that lost energy. A falling or settled river is the one to try if you want to catch a big river pike.

> "We're in!" he shouts, his rod curved over alarmingly, as he connects with a substantial force.

Pike are scavengers. Although they are able to chase individual live fish, that involves expending a lot of energy in a short burst, and they do not always make a clean strike. However, if they go in search of dead fish then the amount of energy used is much less. For this reason, Steve is pinning his hopes on using a deadbait today. Another reason for this is that livebaiting is banned here and he is obliged to abide by local club rules.

Tackle

Steve's thinking on rods is pretty simple: "You need a rod with rings large enough to cope with stop knots and heavy lines. It should have plenty of power to hook and hold big fish in deep water, but I do like it to have a through action."

The reel has a free-running spool facility, which is essential for pike fishing as it allows the predator to pick up the bait and move off with it, even if you might not be directly in attendance at the side of the rod. You just pick up the rod, disengage the free-runner facility and strike into the pike.

As far as terminal tackle is concerned, the Prowla 360 Rotary Paternoster Boom has transformed Steve's pike fishing.

Steve's tackle

Rod: 10ft 6in Greys Prowla Platinum Boat
Reel: Shimano Baitrunner 6000
Float: 23g Fox Predator Stubby Slider
Main line: 50lb Power Pro braid
Terminal: Hardy & Greys Prowla 360 Paternoster Boom, Hardy & Greys Prowla Supa Paternoster trace

At 23lb 5oz, this River Wye pike is a fabulous fish from any river.

"Basically, it has almost eliminated the tangles that were always a feature of these deadbait paternoster rigs," he says. "Plus, the link of weak nylon mono at the lower end of the rig is the part of the tackle that will break if it gets caught in a snag. The rest of the rig will survive intact."

Finally, the trace, when used with the paternoster boom, improves bait presentation, while the red bait flags act as a visual strike target for big predators, while also indicating which points are barbed. The barbed hooks should always be removed first when unhooking fish.

No self-respecting pike angler would go fishing without certain essential tools of the trade and Steve places great emphasis on these specialised items:

Unhooking mat – very important in order to safeguard the fish while on the bank.

Landing net – a large net with a wide mesh will help land big pike safely, especially where the banks are slippery and steep as they often are on the Wye.

Forceps and pliers – different sizes of forceps and pliers make unhooking pike a very straightforward task. Long-nosed pliers are superb for extracting the hooks when they are lodged well inside the toothy mouth of a large pike.

Bite alarm – this allows for audible bite indication to add to the visual indication of the float. Set it to medium sensitivity.

Hot drink – fishing for pike can be a waiting game. Make sure you've plenty of tea, coffee or soup to warm you up on a freezing winter day.

Surface paternoster rig

Steve's rig is described as a 'surface paternoster' and is easy to create.
01 Tie a stop knot on your main line using thick fly-line backing. This should be moved up or down to suit the depth of the water, until the float is visible at the surface.
02 Slide a hard bead onto the line below the stop knot.
03 Add a sliding pike float to the line.
04 Slide on another bead.
05 Attach a Hardy & Greys Prowla 360 Paternoster Boom. These come already attached on an 80cm uptrace of 100lb mono.
06 Attach your trace to the boom arm. Steve uses a Prowla Supa Paternoster trace for this – a trace featuring round-bend trebles mounted on seven-strand 30lb stainless-steel wire. Bait flags help the deadbait stay on the hook as well as adding extra attraction.
07 Finally, tie a 2oz lead on a length of 8lb to 10lb line and attach this to the uptrace. The length of this weaker link will determine how far off the bottom the deadbait sits.

Bait

The next step is to add a bait, and Steve opts for a sizeable dead mackerel.

"There are no hard-and-fast rules about which deadbaits are best for pike," he says, "but I do think that to catch a big fish, you need a big bait! So I am going to opt for the biggest mackerel in the pack and see what happens!"

Steve's other baits included smelt, which have a pungent aroma, and lampreys, which release a lot of blood and can work well on venues like the Wye, which are home to many live lampreys. He hooks the dead fish by pushing the first treble into the eye socket, and the second treble is located past the middle of the bait. These key positions should ensure a clean hook-up.

Take the right gear

01 Plenty of forceps for safe unhooking.

02 Audible bite alarm.

03 A hard-foam rig tube will keep your pike rigs safe.

04 A large landing net with a long handle is a must.

Bait positioning

Finally it's time for Steve to cast out and try to tempt a pike. Looking closely at the river he notices that there is a marked 'crease' between the faster flow and the slower flow closer to the bank. Pike will often hang on the edge of this slower flow to conserve energy, so with this in mind he casts the bait a little way downstream and to the inside edge of that crease area.

The bait is in the river for less than 15 minutes before Steve's bite alarm bursts into life, and he rushes to the rod and engages the spool. He pauses for a few seconds and then heaves the rod up in a strong striking motion to set the trebles.

"We're in!" he shouts, his rod curved over alarmingly, as he connects with a substantial force on the other end. "Feels like a decent fish!" He struggles to control its first surging run, but unless the hooks pull out there's only going to be one winner in this fight; Steve's tackle is more than a match for any predator that swims in British waters.

"The flow in the river is strong here, and this is definitely a big pike, but I'll keep the pressure on it and I think it'll be in the net fairly soon," he

says, just as the pike embarks on another powerful run!

Eventually, Steve is able to guide his prize up the current towards the waiting landing net, but there are a couple of dodgy moments when the big female fish swirls and thrashes explosively on the surface. It's at this point that a big pike can come off!

One more heave and she's in the net. Steve lets out a whoop of delight. "She's definitely a twenty!" he exclaims, as he hoists the magnificent creature up to the top of the bank and safely rests her on the unhooking mat.

He straddles her to prevent her from moving around while the hooks are easily removed. She is quickly weighed and a big, broad smile flashes across Steve's face as he announces her weight at an impressive 23lb 5oz. She's a stunner, with fantastic markings and a sleek, powerful body. What a fish to catch on the first cast of the session!

After a few quick photos, Steve safely returns the lovely predator back to the Wye and, although no more takes follow, he is still buzzing when the morning session finally comes to an end.

A good variety

Always take a good selection of deadbaits. Mackerel, smelt and lampreys are favourites.

When using a paternoster rig, fish with the rod pointing upwards like this, and use a bite alarm for audible indication.

THE NEW REGAL Z AND X BR'S
THERE IS ONE TO SUIT YOU TO A 'T'

The stuff you need for...
pike fishing

Here's a list of the 10 essentials you'll need for a day's predator sport...

01 Wire-meshed glove
Add protection against those razor-sharp teeth when gloving out a fish.

02 Traces
Carry a selection of different snap tackle and lure traces to cover any tactic.

03 Tools
There are a selection of tools to help with removing those large treble hooks.

04 Lines
15lb mono or 30lb braid will cover most pike fishing requirements.

05 Rods
Ensure you choose the right tool for the job for your bait, lure or boat session.

06 Reels
Baitcaster or fixed spool for lures and a large free spool for bait fishing.

07 Accessories
Make sure you carry plenty of swivels, weights, beads and sleeves.

08 Landing net
If you aren't confident enough to lift a fish out by hand, use a big net with large rubber-coated mesh.

09 Unhooking mat
Pike may be vicious, but they are a delicate species that need to be treated with care.

10 Floats
Choose the right float to suit the tactic – livebaiting or deadbaits.

08
09
07
06
10
02
SAVAGE
CARBO FLEX
PREDATOR
STUBBY SINKERS
BAIT FLAGS
TRACE CRIMP COVER
PREDATOR CARBO FLEX
7 STRAND CARBON COATED STAINLESS STEEL LEADER
TITANIUM
30lb
E-SOX
28lb

EUROPE'S TOP FISHING MAGAZINES ARE AVAILABLE ON YOUR iPHONE, iPAD OR ANDROID DEVICE. . .

SIMPLY SEARCH THE RELEVANT MAGAZINE TITLE

(ALL THE FEATURES, NO PAPER CUTS)

powered by

ALSO LIVE ON THE ANDROID MARKET!

Think again about zander

It's the thinking angler who catches most fish. Ask **Duncan Charman**, who has come up with an unusual approach for fickle zander.

Duncan Charman

Hometown:
Aldershot
Occupation: Wedding photographer, angling guide and Korum consultant.

Zander! The name is enough to strike fear into the hearts of many coarse anglers. Seen as voracious predators, ruthlessly hunting in packs and attacking anything in their path, zander have been hated and adored in equal measure since they first appeared in UK waters back in the 1960s. Since being introduced into the Great Ouse system, zander have spread widely and can now be found in many waters – both still and running – across England.

But after the initial furore, stemming from the imbalance created by the introduction of a new predator, zander have now acquired a place in the ecosystem of any water where they are found. They're here to stay and I, for one, have been making the most of them ever since they appeared in some southern fisheries not far from where I live.

Bury Hill Fisheries is a good example of a water where zander quite happily thrive among the huge shoals of bream, tench and other species that reside in the fishery's main lake.

Once the summer's over, I like to target the zander here, and just lately I've been experimenting with methods as far away from traditional predator fishing as you could imagine. Waggler and feeder fishing for zander – oh yes! Join me as I spend a day at Bury Hill and you might just want to think again about your zander fishing…

Tough conditions

As the first rays of sunlight shine through the far-bank trees, I lengthen my stride along the path to a swim that has supplied a couple of red-letter days for me the previous week. However, deep down I know that today will be harder.

What can only be described as a brief Indian summer has drifted over the country at a time when we should be pulling on the thermal

Venue file

Bury Hill Fisheries, The Boathouse, Old Bury Hill, Westcott, Dorking, Surrey RH4 3JU
Contact: Tel 01306 877540; website *www.buryhillfisheries. co.uk*; e-mail *info@ buryhillfisheries.com*
Day tickets: Adults £11.50, concessions Mon-Sat £8.50 from the shop
Facilities: Bait and tackle shop, café, tuition available, match bookings taken
Opening times: Open every day except Christmas Day and Boxing Day. Weekdays 7am-sunset. Weekends and bank holidays sunrise (5.30am earliest) to sunset

It might look like casting a feeder for bream, but Duncan Charman has something altogether 'toothier' on his mind.

underwear. Now it's gone and, worse still, a cool breeze chills my left cheek as I walk the bank, indicating that the wind is blowing from the most unfavoured direction possible – the east.

Arriving at permanent Peg 42 in the early morning, I know I have to get the rods out as quickly as possible. Zander feed with confidence when light levels are low and within seconds I have two low-resistance 1oz running rigs with hair-rigged sardine sections positioned around 30 yards out. Despite the conditions, I'm expecting a bite quite quickly, but after 20 minutes there's no action. I wind in, refresh the hook baits and then cast out slightly further in the hope that the disturbance caused by the splash of the lead and bait might induce a bite, but once again the bobbins fail to move. Today's conditions are proving impossible!

Sensory system

Two sessions the previous week yielded 45 fish including zander to 12lb 13oz with many being caught on the waggler. Today, it's obvious this isn't going to happen. What I need is a technique that will stir even the most lethargic zander into feeding. It just has to be the swimfeeder!

Although zander are brilliantly adapted to catch prey by sight, they need to use all of their sensory system to find their food in the coloured water of the main lake at Bury Hill and it's their ability to locate a food source by taste that I have based my new tactic on.

My running rigs failed to produce, so it's time to try the feeder rod, using a reasonably powerful rod that will cope with a heavy main line as well as being able to set a hook into the hard mouth of a zander, a match-sized feeder reel and 12lb line. The line has 50 per cent less stretch than standard monofilament and will register any small knocks clearly on the quivertip.

I have every confidence in my setup; now it's just a case of getting a few bites! After positioning everything neatly on the platform around me

No, your eyes aren't deceiving you; it's a zander and not a bream being brought to Duncan's net.

ready for my first cast with a feeder, I'm suddenly taken by surprise as my alarm sounds. The yellow bottle top indicator slowly rises on the rod that's been left out. I rush to get to the rod before the line tightens and I strike just as it reaches the top but nothing is pulling back and I know I've just missed my first chance.

Time for the feeder

Knowing that zander hate resistance and will immediately drop bait if any is felt, I have modified my mesh feeder to take a running clip so that the ring sits upright off the bottom. This runs freely on the main line and is buffeted by a quick-change bead, a brilliant little device that allows me to replace the trace quickly and cast out again

Tackle tip

Duncan always uses a bottle-top indicator when zander fishing with an alarm.

Duncan's feed

01 Sonubaits' Supercrush Green groundbait holds everything together.

02 Mix the groundbait and add some of the fish pieces.

03 Hair-rigged, frozen sardine pieces are used for hook bait.

04 Duncan's fish pieces are kept frozen in a Gardner cool bag.

Tackle tip

Note the wide rod rest. When he gets a bite, Duncan moves his rods to the end of the rest before striking.

their irresistible taste into the water. The next step is to fill the feeder. Into this goes a liquidised concoction of sardines, sprats and mackerel all firmed together with some Sonubaits Supercrush Green groundbait. As the feeder lands on water, an oil slick can be instantly seen on the surface. If this doesn't work, then nothing will.

I have positioned myself so the rod rests comfortably across my lap. My rod rest is a wide padded one, which will allow me to move the rod along it when I get a bite. If the tip is still going by the time the rod reaches the other end of the rest, I strike.

After 10 minutes it's time to wind in again and I strike the sardine section off so that I leave a few larger items within my swim as well as loads of tiny fish pieces from the feeder. Refreshing the hook bait and refilling the feeder, I cast out again. Again, nothing happens, so I continue to cast at regular intervals until, an hour into the routine, the tip jerks forward then slowly bends. It looks for all the world like a bream bite, and I move the rod along the rest before making a strong sweeping strike to set the hook.

I have caught carp, bream and pike here on sardine sections, so I really don't know what's on the hook, but after a spirited fight that feels 10 times better than on my 1.5lb test-curve rods, a big, ghostly eye appears among a spray of water. It's my first ever zander on the quivertip-and-feeder combination.

while the fish is still in the landing net – useful if I'm catching fast.

I have a couple of traces with frozen sardine sections already mounted in my cool box, so after netting a fish I can simply clip one on and recast, leaving me to unhook, weigh and photograph my catch.

Zander feed in packs and it's often the case that if you catch one fish, then you will get a few bites soon after, so by being organised and getting a bait back out in your swim as soon as possible, you will maximise your chances. To the bead I add a 15in hook link with a size 8 hook and a 1½in flexible braided hair.

Look at the eye on that critter! No wonder zander feed largely by sight. This one weighed 5lb.

Sardines

The sun is now above the far-bank trees and the early morning chill is replaced by unseasonably warm air. The breeze has all but disappeared, leaving a lake that's still and uninviting. Taking a sardine from the cool box, I cut a ½in section from its body and then push a gated baiting needle through its frozen flesh before attaching the hair. Pulling the needle back, I then secure the section on by using several boilie stops attached together.

The reason for using frozen sardines is that all the blood and guts remain intact when casting and then, once submerged, will dissolve releasing

Duncan's feeder tackle

Rod: Korum Precision 12ft Multi-Feeder
Reel: Preston Innovations PXR 4000
Line: 12lb Direct Mono
Feeder: Modified Korum Medium 30g Mesh
Hook: Korum S3 barbless
Rod rest: Preston Dutch Feeder

Releasing the quick-change bead, I quickly attach another trace and recast in the hope of a repeat performance and almost immediately another bite develops, but unfortunately this time I don't make contact. With the bait back out I go to unhook the small zander in my net, only to find that the hook has come out by itself, something that often happens when using a longish hair as almost every fish is hooked just inside the mouth.

Another bite

It doesn't take long before the quivertip jerks forward then pulls round. A strong strike makes contact and the fight is from a better fish, a zander of around 4lb. Anyone who reckons zander don't fight wants to fish like this as they give a good account of themselves right up until you net them.

No-one else is catching. The conditions are cruel and I can only assume that the zander are now feeding after dark, laying up all day before

becoming active once more later. As the afternoon progresses I'm confident that a few more bites will materialise and that the bigger fish will switch on and, as expected, late in the afternoon the tip once again sweeps round and a far bigger fish takes line from the clutch.

This one weighs around 5lb. They're getting bigger! Now anglers are beginning to leave, but I know the last hour is often the most productive and with just a few minutes left before sunset, I connect with a fish that just doesn't want to come to the net. I almost convince myself it's a carp due to its power but once again an angry eye stares at me as I guide a fine fish over the landing net. At 8lb 1oz, it brings an end to a very enjoyable day.

I'm convinced that my repeated casting with the feeder has bought me a few extra bites. Building a swim in such a manner has brought back memories of my match days and once again it's a tactic from the match world that has been modified and brought into the specimen scene that has produced the goods.

Forceps are a must for unhooking zander.

Duncan's five top zander tips

01 Take any fish offcuts home and liquidise them to produce a groundbait.
02 Don't sit on motionless rods; frequent casting often brings instant bites.
03 Fishing tight lines will result in dropped runs. If using bobbins, use light ones, on a long drop.
04 Use frozen fish sections on the hook. They keep blood and guts intact and won't fall apart on casting.
05 Strike almost immediately and if you miss the run cast back out into the same position.

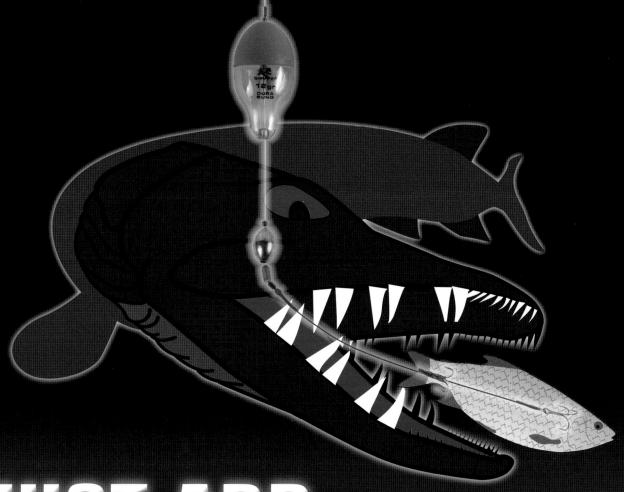

Surface sizzlers

Seven styles of top-water lure to help you enjoy some explosive predator action.

Prop Bait

These feature one or two propellers and create a massive disturbance when drawn across the surface layers. They can be continually retrieved or worked through the water by jerking and leaving them for a few seconds. Some have great names, too, like the Cripple Killer, Devil's Horse, Tiny Torpedo and the Cisco Kid Topper (pictured).

Popper

Wooden or plastic lures with a concave head which creates a 'popping' sound when you jerk the rod. They come in endless sizes and colours, and are good for fishing alongside surface weed and reed beds or above sub-surface weed. Pictured are the Rapala Firetiger Skitter Pop (right), and a big-eyed silver Bullet Popper from Double MM.

Jitterbug

Another classic from across the Pond that weaves and 'splurts' across the surface layers on a slow retrieve, making a 'glub, glub' sound, and which triggers a predator's naturally aggressive behaviour. It's actually a type of crawler but is worth a mention in its own right and is regarded in the States as a superb night-time lure as well as being effective in daylight.

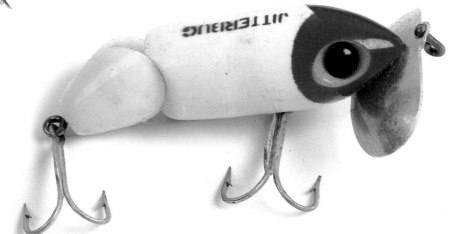

Crawler

Pictured is the Heddon Crazy Crawler, an all-time American classic, with a red head and flexible front fins that create havoc, throwing water all over the place as the lure effectively swims (or crawls) across the surface. One of the easiest lures to use and brilliant fun! Also very effective at night.

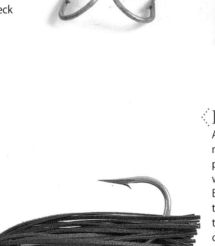

Frog

These are very realistic, usually made from soft rubber and often include a weed guard to allow them to be fished through lilies and weeds. The Berkley Frenzy Power Pop has a wooden body and unique curly legs, which kick out and retract just like those of a real frog! It comes in several patterns, including Leopard Frog (pictured). The other pictured frog is the all-rubber Rubberneck Froggie which comes with a weed guard.

Buzzbait

A top-water category lure that takes a bit more work as it does not float. As the lure is pulled through the water the blades chop the water's surface and create quite a commotion. Buzzbaits are similar in physical appearance to spinnerbaits. They are built with a blade that resembles a butterfly with its wings outstretched and is cupped on the tips. Two-bladed aluminium buzz blades are the most popular, with silver or chrome the most common colour.

Do-Nothing Lure

As you would imagine, these don't do a lot until the angler puts some action into them by jerking the rod from side to side and twitching them across the top – so they are best fished with a stiffish rod. However, they also catch fish on a steady, slow retrieve. The lure pictured is The Ghost and is a rattling, hollow, soft-plastic lure with a double hook designed for fishing around heavy vegetation mats, and is very good on overcast days.

Give your pike some TLC!

Despite appearances, the pike is one of Britain's most vulnerable coarse fish and a little tender loving care will go a long way. **Jon Neafcy** offers some timely advice on looking after them.

Did you know that many responsible anglers are put off pike fishing because they are scared of catching one? Whether it's handling the fish on the bank, deep hooking them or being hurt by their teeth, some of the issues associated with pike fishing are enough to deter many people. However, when carried out in the right way, piking is one of the most exciting and exhilarating of all types of fishing.

A pike's design as a predatory hunter is perfection itself, having remained the same for millions of years. Take the pike out of its watery kingdom onto the bank, though, and it is very vulnerable; deep-hooked and badly handled fish can easily die. Pike stocks are precious and a dwindling pike population in a venue through pollution or bad angling practices is not easily replenished.

Pike, unlike carp and some other coarse species, are most likely to be 'natural'. They will not have been imported from other countries and if those in your chosen venue die, they cannot be replaced. Pike are not generally commercially available from fish farms and a 10-pounder will be several years old.

Jon Neafcy
Occupation: Regional manager for DHL parcel delivery
Hometown: Wigan
Personal-best pike: 35lb 1oz from Lake Windermere, Cumbria

The toothy pike appears ferocious on the outside, but is delicate on the inside.

Add to this the fact that pike are the first fish to suffer if a water becomes polluted, and you'll hopefully realise that pike are extremely vulnerable creatures, perhaps more so than any other freshwater fish. Their fearsome reputation hides an extremely delicate interior!

So how can you go about pike fishing in the knowledge that your quarry will be unharmed? Is it as simple as, say, replacing a braided hook link and boilie with a wire trace and half a mackerel? Most definitely not…

Tackle

Here's a rundown of the tackle you'll need…

Rod and reel: Any decent, strong carp-type rod and reel will be fine

Main line: Minimum 18lb mono – I use Daiwa Infinity HD or Duo. The key is to regularly check your line for wear and damage, and replace as necessary

Wire trace: A pike's teeth necessitate a wire trace of 40lb or 50lb. Many ready-made ones are available and these are generally very good

Hooks: Semi-barbless trebles are the ones to use. Go for size 6 for small-to-medium baits

Weak link: This is important when legering and float fishing paternoster-style with a boom. Your leger weight is attached to a length of line weaker than the main line that will break if the weight becomes snagged, so you won't lose your rig and, more importantly, you won't leave a baited hook in the water.

Bite alarms

Most bite alarms aren't suited to pike fishing with an open bail arm and drop-off bobbin. This is because once the line is pulled from the bobbin clip and the line is free running the alarm will suffer from line skip, with the line likely to pass above or over the wheel without turning it. Consequently the alarm will not continue to sound as the fish takes line.

If you must use this type of indicator don't fish with an open bail arm, use the reel's free-spool facility coupled with a suitable visual-indicator bobbin, although there is a school of thought that says that the resistance can lead to dropped runs, particularly on pressured waters.

The only front alarm I know that works with open-bail-arm fishing is the Delkim, as it

You must use strong tackle!

Make sure your hooks and other terminal tackle are strong and reliable.

The 'traditional' pike season runs from October 1st to March 14th and those are good dates to stick to for pike fishing.

A fine double, perfectly held by Jon Neafcy for a photo.

How to unhook a pike

01 After landing, place the net on your unhooking mat, turn the pike over and gently 'straddle' it with legs either side.

02 Insert the fingers of one hand either side of the gills, finding the place where there are no teeth or gill rakers.

03 Exert slight upward pressure, which will open the pike's mouth.

04 You can now unhook the fish using your specialist needle-nosed pliers or forceps.

doesn't work off a wheel.

The other type of suitable bite alarm is the drop-off or back-biter. This attaches to the rear bankstick and sounds either when the line is pulled from the clip, causing the arm to fall, or when it drops back. Whichever remote you use, always test it and make sure it is within range. Never rely solely on a remote; if it lets you down it could mean a deep-hooked pike.

Other tools for the job

Landing net: Use at least a 42in model. This might seem a little on the large side but you need to use a net that will easily hold the biggest of pike.

Large unhooking mat/weigh sling: Use a combination version as it minimises handling of the fish. You'll also need long – 10in to 12in – needle-nosed pliers.

When to fish

The 'traditional' pike season runs from October 1st to March 14th and those are good dates to stick to for pike fishing. The problem with summer piking is that pike will suffer if you catch them from small, shallow venues that will often be low in oxygen.

However, there would be no problems when pike fishing in summer on a big, deep, northern glacial lake or Scottish loch as the water temperature is lower in these venues.

Handling and unhooking

The best advice to pike fishing newcomers is to net everything – don't try to 'chin' a pike unless you are competent in doing so.

Once the pike is in the landing net, place the net on your unhooking mat, turn the pike upside down and gently 'straddle' the pike,

Treat cuts fast!

Cuts from pike teeth like this must be treated immediately to prevent infection.

with your legs either side, to prevent it moving.

Now insert the fingers of one hand either side of the gills into the chin, finding the 'safe' bit where there are no teeth or gill rakers. Special gloves are available if you are worried about this, but I don't use them.

Having inserted your fingers exert slight upwards pressure, which will open the pike's mouth and allow you to unhook the fish using your specialist needle-nosed pliers or forceps. You may need to pull the trace taut to help you get the hooks out.

If the pike is hooked in the throat or stomach, then you are not striking soon enough.

How to hold a pike

So, you've been fortunate enough to hook and land a big pike, and now you want a quick photo. Here's how to do it:

After weighing it, place the weigh sling down on the ground. If it's a combined mat/sling, that will be fine. If not, place it down on a mat, lay the fish out in front of you on the mat, insert one hand under the chin of the fish, place your other hand by the anal fin and roll the pike gently onto your hands.

Now lift it and quickly get your photo. On

Eight key steps to avoid deep hooking

01 Good bite indication coupled with quick striking is the key to not deep hooking pike.

02 When you're float fishing, always keep a good check on the float.

03 Never set the float too far overdepth or you won't see a bite early enough.

04 Never freeline, as this is a method prone to deep hooking.

05 Always ensure a good indication setup is used.

06 Tighten the drag on your reel so that the clutch doesn't scream when you hit into a fish.

07 To strike a run, wind down quickly until you feel resistance and then pull the rod back over your shoulder.

08 Don't leave runs too long; hooking pike in the throat or gut is not good practice and could lead to a dead fish.

completion, put the fish back into the sling and return it quickly and gently to the water. The whole photographing process can be achieved in very little time but even so, with every pike you catch, ask yourself whether you really need to record it on camera for posterity.

Helping hand

The Pike Anglers' Club of Great Britain (*www.pacgb.co.uk*) and the Pike Anglers' Alliance for Scotland (*www.esoxecosse.com*) are excellent clubs.

Both operate on a regional level, with excellent websites containing plenty of free information. These clubs are the main voice of pike angling, and without them pike and pike fishing would suffer.

I have been a PAC member since I was a junior and both associations contain anglers of all abilities, from seasoned veterans to novices. However, the real key to learning is getting out there and fishing for yourself in a responsible manner.

How to return a pike

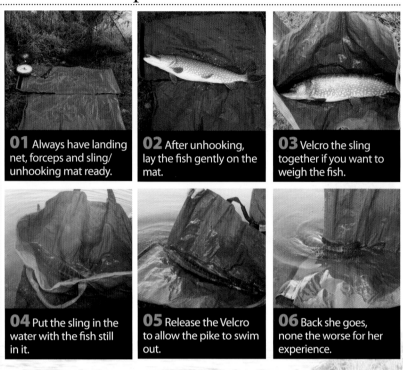

01 Always have landing net, forceps and sling/unhooking mat ready.

02 After unhooking, lay the fish gently on the mat.

03 Velcro the sling together if you want to weigh the fish.

04 Put the sling in the water with the fish still in it.

05 Release the Velcro to allow the pike to swim out.

06 Back she goes, none the worse for her experience.

Pike can be caught in subzero temperatures. Note the dual alarm and drop-bobbin combination.

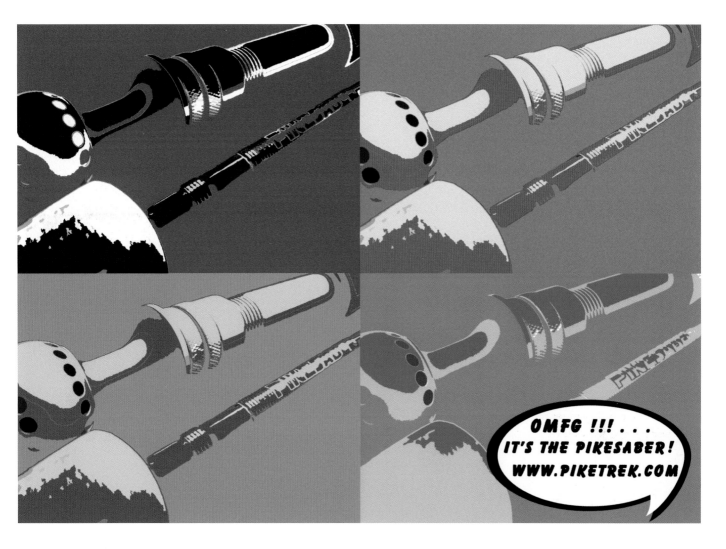

©2008Rapala

Glidin' Rap®
Available in 12, 15cm
& 7 Colours

Banded Black

Olive Flash

Turns predators into prey on contact.

Introducing the New Glidin' Rap, it's time to turn the tables.

rapala.com

Follow Rapala on **facebook** www.facebook.com/rapalauk

Mick Brown

The UK's top predator angler recalls a very special day in the Baltic Sea.

Surroundings don't come more inspiring to a pike angler than the Baltic Sea off the coast of Finland on an early spring day. Fishing around the many large and small islands by both casting and trolling lures was an experience I'll always savour. As a guest of Rapala, I was there for three days along with several other international anglers who had contributed work to a Rapala publication. We lodged in a log cabin on a rocky island and ate nothing but fish – cod, sea trout, salmon and perch.

Because the water was so cold, just 1°C or so, our lures had to be trolled precisely within inches of the bottom. This took intense concentration and those who adhered to the principle caught, while those who couldn't manage it caught very little. I can't describe the pleasure of working at getting a hit while the guides with us talked glibly of 30-pounders caught and 40-pounders lost in the sea around us.

It was hard to take in the fact that pike lived in saltwater. I had to taste the water to prove it was, and believe me it tasted as salty as any I've swallowed on the beach at Skegness!

We didn't catch huge numbers of pike but enough to keep us busy, with most being low to mid 'doubles', plus a few bonus perch. Knowing this opportunity wouldn't come again, I really focused on what I was doing and was taking my fair share of the catch, which was shared with 'Piking Pirate' Gord Burton and Jan Eggers, the famous Dutch pike angler.

Quietly going about my business, I was totally engrossed in making sure that my 18cm Magnum lure worked as close to the bottom as possible, using occasional contact with the bottom as my guide while the boatman kept us informed of the depth from his echo sounder.

Suddenly the rod rammed round. However, instead of a pike surging away, I was locked up solid! It had to be a snag – or so I thought! The boatman protested when I asked him to stop, telling me it was a sand bottom and impossible to snag up. Convinced he was wrong, I eventually got him to stop and we drifted back to get above the 'snag', which seemed to be rising in the water, feeling rather like an old log. It was a fish! Perhaps the icy water and the shock of being hooked had numbed the senses of the old warrior, having lived for probably 15 years or more without seeing a hook.

Despite the Magnum barely hanging on to her jaw by one point, it seemed a formality to lift her into the boat.

Then she woke up! How the lure stayed in place during the following five minutes I'll never know, but it did. When she finally gave up, Gordy chinned her and the hook slipped out as he swung her over the high side of the big trolling boat.

It was an awesome pike, long and athletic and with a wicked jaw. She looked much bigger, but I was more than happy that the scales read exactly 26lb. How many herrings had she scoffed in her years chasing the big shoals that inhabit the area? I slept well in the cabin that night, but not before celebrating with a large helping of cod and a glass or two of whisky!

Mick Brown

Hometown: Market Deeping, Lincolnshire
Sponsors: Shimano, Rapala and Dynamite Baits

Mick Brown is best known as a successful predator angler, having caught more than 300 pike over 20lb and 16 UK catfish in excess of 60lb. He enjoys many other styles of fishing, ranging from float fishing for tench to fly fishing for trout. Now he is getting excited about the launch of his new book and his new job with the recently formed Shimano-Normark joint venture.

Mick's 26lb pike rounded off a great day's fishing in the Baltic Sea.

Ten ways to catch...
perch

For many, these greedy little blighters were probably the first fish they ever caught when they were young. Here are 10 tips to help you target them on any venue.

Lures

1 Many anglers think that perch only attack small lures. That's not the case, as plenty of big specimens fall to 3in to 4in lures meant for pike.

Red maggots

2 Smaller perch shoal together, and by feeding and fishing red maggots you will get them into a feeding frenzy, which can attract better specimens.

Blockend feeder

3 One of the best ways to attract a big perch to the hook bait is by using a tiny, small-holed feeder loaded with a chopped lobworm and a few red maggots.

Worm-soil groundbait

4 If you buy your worms in bulk, don't throw away the medium they come in – it smells of worms and makes a great groundbait to feed with chopped baits.

Floats

5 A perch will quickly drop a bait if it feels the slightest resistance, so try and fish with floats that are just buoyant enough to support the bait.

Livebaits

6 Small livebaits tend to attract bigger stripeys, particularly from stillwaters. The most popular baits are float-fished small roach and gudgeon.

Features

7 Perch feed by ambushing their prey, so if a big specimen is your quarry look for landing stages, boats and underwater snags, along with dense reed beds.

Lobworms

8 These are the number-one bait for perch.

Casters

9 Perch love casters, especially on canals and rivers. They regularly home in on baits meant for roach and skimmers.

Syringe

10 A legered, popped-up worm is a super deep-water tactic. However, if you are going to use a syringe, please be aware of the safety aspects.

The livebait float
RIG

This rig is ideal for targeting pike on lakes and slow-moving rivers. It's an incredibly simple setup that allows you to explore every level of the venue you're fishing. Used with a dumpy-type float, any wind will push the bait around causing the bait to react enticingly against the pull. It's a rig that can be fished from the bank or, where possible, a boat. Here's a breakdown of the items you will need and how to put the rig together.

What you need

1 x predator-style stop
1 x small bead
1 x dumpy-style float
1 x free-running weight
1 x buffer bead
1 x quick-change swivel
1 x large sleeve
1 x 20in wire trace
2 x size 6 semi-barbed treble hooks

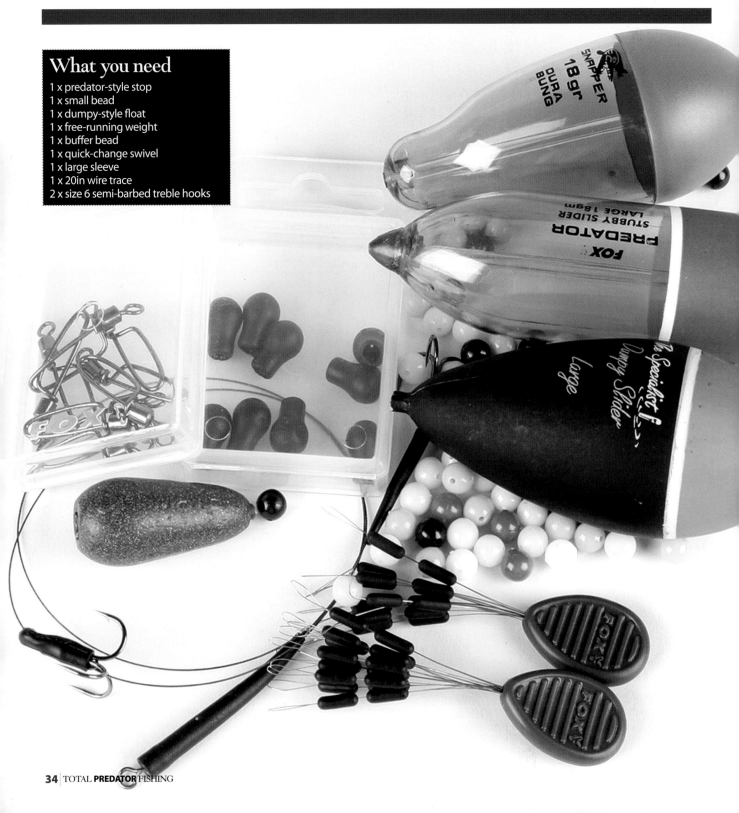

How to make the rig

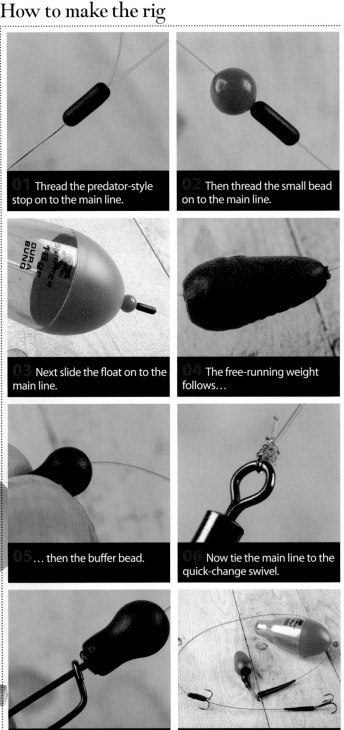

01 Thread the predator-style stop on to the main line.

02 Then thread the small bead on to the main line.

03 Next slide the float on to the main line.

04 The free-running weight follows…

05 … then the buffer bead.

06 Now tie the main line to the quick-change swivel.

07 Slide the bead over the swivel to protect the knot.

08 Finally, attach the trace for your livebait.

How to attach the livebait

01 Take the top treble and push the barbed hook in close to the dorsal fin.

02 Then place the barbed hook of the second treble close to the pectoral fin.

The fishing depth is set using a predator stop and bead above the sliding float

Main line is 15lb mono or 30lb braid

Free-running weight rests against a large buffer bead

The wire trace is attached to the rig using a quick-change swivel

Attach the hooks so that the livebait swims naturally

The 20in trace is made from 30lb coated wire

Soft-lure revolution

Using the right lure can make or break your predator success. Savage Gear's **Rasmus Ovesen** explains how the new Soft 4Play lures are versatile… and deadly.

A s a predator fisherman, success is very often contingent on versatility and finesse. Presentation and fishing tactics can be pivotal but a lot of times, the right lure is what saves the day.

Lure fishing for pike, perch, and zander is great fun and at its best can be both uncomplicated and hectic.

However, the opposite can hold true as well, and once in a while we experience days when these superior predators seem lethargic and unco-operative. We all have a magical lure or two that seems to be able to save the day, when all else fails. But what we secretly hope for is to find that one lure, that does the trick every time.

The new Savage Gear 4Play lure might be that lure. It comes in 9.5cm, 13cm, and 19cm versions, and what really makes it interesting is that it can be fished in so many different and unique ways that it covers just about any fishing situation – no matter how challenging it is, and no matter where the fish feed in the column of water.

It comes in two versions, a loose body version and a 'ready-to-fish' version which comes mounted on a wire skeleton with a treble hook. Furthermore, a whole series of jigheads, off-set hooks, and Lip Skulls have been developed to further improve versatility.

The new Savage Gear Soft 4Play lure differs from others in its design and fishing possibilities. It is based on the extremely successful 4Play

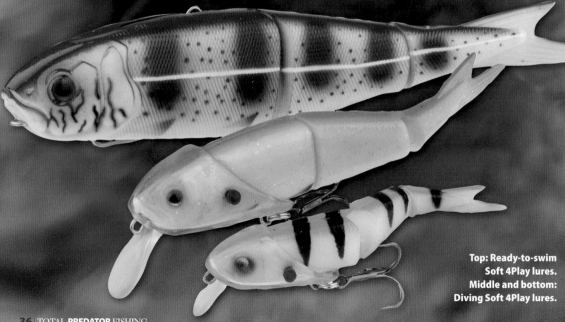

Top: Ready-to-swim Soft 4Play lures. Middle and bottom: Diving Soft 4Play lures.

Rasmus Ovesen

Hometown:
Gadstrup, Denmark
Occupation:
Marketing
co-ordinator,
Svendsen Sport

**Another big
perch comes
to the net.**

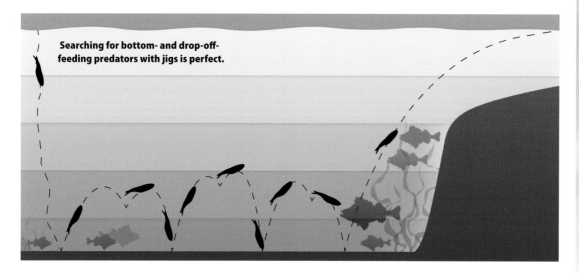

Searching for bottom- and drop-off-feeding predators with jigs is perfect.

Perfectly attached and ready to fish.

hard lures and imitates a small fish very convincingly.

The Soft 4Play is different from other lures in a number of ways. First of all, it has a jointed body consisting of three sections that makes it wiggle and twist just like a real fish. Secondly, and unlike most other fish-imitating jigs, the Soft 4Play lure is a loose body lure, which means that it can be mounted in several different and very interesting ways.

Bottom fishing

Pike, perch and zander can be found near the bottom at varying depths throughout most of the year. Especially when water temperatures are relatively low during winter and spring, the fish can be found close to the bottom and near drop-offs. Getting to them obviously requires lures that work the depths of the rivers and lakes that harbour these fish, and jigs have been a long-time favourite for this type of fishing. They plummet to the bottom quickly and can be fished just above the lake and river bottoms without snagging up at all.

For bottom fishing, the Soft 4Play lure mounted on a ball jig head is snag-free, and can be fished with rapid jerks or with slow pulls, depending on the circumstances. Simply retrieving the lure slowly along the bottom with a few bottom impacts thrown in here and there can be effective, especially in cold water.

In general, however, it's difficult to do it wrong – and the strikes are unpredictable and sudden. Use braided line such as the Savage Gear HD line, and keep tension on the line on the drop. This is important since a lot of times the fish will strike on the drop – to them it obviously appears that the little 'bait fish' they are stalking is fleeing towards the bottom for shelter and protection – and this calls for a rapid strike.

Pike and perch usually completely engulf the lure, whereas zander quite often act differently. They hunt down bait fish and hammer them once

Rasmus Ovesen with a Soft 4Play-caught zander.

or twice with their sharp teeth only to pick up them up mortally wounded shortly after. When fishing for zander with the lures, keeping the line taut at all times is pivotal. The lures have real fish-meat density, and quite often zander will strike them several times before settling on the final attack.

These lures are good for drop-shotting, a branch of the sport which is becoming popular.

When a zander tests and strikes the lure, try dropping it to the bottom, twitch it subtly and then do a long slow motion upwards. This will imitate the last struggling escape of a wounded fish, and it will trigger a rapid response.

These lures are good for drop-shotting, a branch of the sport which is becoming increasingly popular. By mounting the lure sideways with the hook protruding out of the side of the lure body, you can make the lure flutter and twitch in all directions and not just up and down, like the usual soft lures used for drop shotting. This is a clear advantage, since fishing lures vertically can tend to make presentation quite static.

Ready-to-fish lures
Especially during the summer, when both pike and perch can be rather lethargic, and the weeds and reeds protrude high up in the water,

Try loading your lure with a herring strip for added attraction.

Where to buy them

Soft 4Play lures are distributed by Svendsen Sport, and they come in three different sizes (9.5cm, 13cm and 19cm) with the addition of a 25cm version coming out in 2012. Colours available include Dirty Silver, Perch, Firetiger, Rainbow Smolt, Dirty Roach, Fungus Roach, Zander, Fluo Orange & Gold, Smolt, and Pearl Silver. For more information and to request your nearest dealer, please contact Svendsen Sport A/S: *info@svendsen-sport.com*

fishing in the top region of the water can be very effective.

The 'ready-to-fish' version of the lure, fitted with a metal skeleton and a single treble hook, has a fairly slow sink rate making it perfect for fishing in the upper column of the water.

When retrieved slowly, it has a subtle kicking action, and with some radical and sudden pulls thrown in, you can make the lure jerk from one side to the other – something that perfectly imitates a frightened fish trying to escape.

Just be ready for some lightning-fast strikes, because the pike especially will lie await below – ready to make one of their incredibly quick trademark attacks.

The Soft 4Play can also be fished in one of the Savage Gear Lip Skulls, which have been designed specifically for this purpose. They are lip-mounted skulls with a single treble hook, into which the Soft 4Play lures are fastened with a safety pin. Once inserted and fastened, the Soft 4Play can be fished just like a regular wobbler, and depending on the speed of retrieve, it will work its way down two to three metres in the water.

Surface fishing

For top-water fishing, the Soft 4Play lures can be mounted on offset hooks – with the hook point buried just below the soft skin of the lure, ready to penetrate when the fish bites down on it. With this type of mounting, the lures can be fished through lily pads, close to reeds and weeds, and even through sunken trees and branches.

Weight can be added to the offset hooks before mounting the lure, but without any added weight it can be fished just below the surface or in the surface film like a jerk bait, and you will be in for some extremely visual takes with lots of roaring splashes. This type of fishing can be especially good during late summer, and both pike and perch will hit the lures with reckless abandon.

So give these lures a try if you want some serious predator action now!

Top European lure angler Mads Grosell with a summer pike.

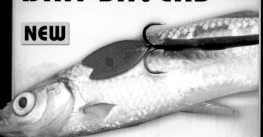

Predator Q&A

Total Predator Fishing answers those nagging predator queries.

Q Is rod and reel choice important?

A Absolutely! If you use a short rod of up to six feet long then a baitcasting, multiplier-type reel is perfect for casting and working lures that don't have to travel too far. Once you move on to longer rods then a standard fixed-spool reel will allow you to cover greater distances on larger venues.

If you are trying a method known as 'jerkbaiting', in which you have to impart the movement into a large wooden lure, then a very stiff rod is critical.

Q Why do pike anglers use braided lines of a heavier breaking strain than mono lines?

A Most pike anglers use mono lines from 12 to 15lb breaking strain. If you look at the equivalent breaking strain in braid it is extremely low in diameter. These low-diameter braids are perfect for light techniques like jig fishing and spinning with small lures, but when used on bait rods and casting relatively heavy deadbaits they are very troublesome. Tangles and wind knots are common and you can easily cut into your fingers when miscasting or striking against a slipping clutch.

Choose a braid of similar diameter to your mono. This reduces these problems, and adds extra strength. As a rough rule of thumb, the equivalent diameter in braid almost doubles the strength of mono. This offers obvious advantages towards the safety of the pike through minimising chances of breakages. The thicker braid is more durable and offers better abrasion resistance.

Q I have a 6ft spinning rod and multiplier reel. Should I load the reel with braid of mono, and what breaking strain?

A A braided line is the best choice here. The lack of stretch compared to that in mono means that bite detection and efficient striking is vastly superior. Your rod should be marked with a casting-weight rating. This is nearly always printed on the rod itself. A very light spinning rod would be rated something like 5g to 20g, which means that this is the weight range of the lures the rod is able to safely cast without risk of damaging it. The lures themselves are rated with their weight in a similar way so it's easy to choose lures that will match your rod.

A more typical 'general-purpose' lure rod would be rated in the region of 20g to 60g casting weight and a heavy-duty rod might be rated at 40g to 100g casting weight. Clearly, each rod needs using with different line strengths to cater for the lures it is used for.

As a rule of thumb then, use a 15lb to 20lb braid for a 5g to 20g rod. 20lb to 30lb braid is best on a general-purpose 20g to 60g rod, while a heavy-duty lure rod will need anything from 30lb to 50lb braid. If you tend to use lures at the heavier end of the range for the rods and/or the swims you fish are snaggy, then opt for lines at the stronger end of the scale.

Q Is it true that pike will take a lure when it is not interested in a live or deadbait?

A It is a fact that a pike can be tempted to take a lure when it refuses a deadbait even if it is not that hungry. Why it would refuse a well-presented livebait is a mystery, though.

Pike aren't a difficult fish to catch for two main reasons. First of all, it is in their nature to be inquisitive and attack anything that moves and they think they can eat. When something moves in their territory, it is hard for them not to react unless they are restrained for any

reason. A lure will not always work as pike can become really lethargic due to low water temperatures, digesting recent meals or sometimes they are wary of the angler. Very often a lure will raise a reaction, though. Knowing this should make you think more deeply about lure presentation as, most times, any old retrieve will not be good enough and so lure choice and how it's worked is of paramount importance.

At other times, a pike will attack anything that enters its territory with no intention of eating it. They will simply be making the point that they are annoyed with this intrusion and they will 'see it off', perhaps snapping at it in the process.

Snow patrol

There's been a fresh fall of snow, so do you let it put you off that planned pike trip, or, like **Luke Broderick** and **Dean Brook**, do you pack the gear and get down to the river!

Venue file

River Wharfe
Location: Tadcaster, Yorkshire
Tickets: Members only. Adults £43. Juniors £12. Intermediates and OAPs £19.
Contact: 0776 507 5582

Luke Broderick and Dean Brook love a challenge, and that means getting out onto the bank regardless of what the British weather throws at them. This trip began with the world carpeted with white, but that did not deter the fishing friends, and soon they were in the car and heading off to the water's edge, deadbaits in hand.

"There's something magical, rare and special about a day's piking in the snow," explained 30Plus-sponsored Luke. "Everything takes on a different appearance. It's like fishing in another world."

A total whiteout would deter many anglers from leaving home, but not Luke and Dean.

"We love it!" grinned Luke, as he trudged through ankle-deep, newly fallen snow from the car park at the top of the hill that lead steeply down to the River Wharfe at Easedyke, just above Tadcaster in Yorkshire.

Light and warm

In conditions like these, Luke and Dean travelled as light as possible, but they also wrapped up warm.

The right choice of clothing and footwear makes all the difference when you are out in the depths of winter, but when heavy snow comes into the equation, it's even more important to have 100 per cent waterproof jackets, plus a bib 'n' brace and thick-soled boots.

"Yes, and a flask of hot soup or tea and some sandwiches will keep your internal engine burning," said Luke. "This leads to you being able to dedicate yourself to the task in hand, which is simply to tempt a pike to take the bait. Any size pike will do on days like this. It's all about having fun and enjoying the special atmosphere that a snowy scene adds to a day's fishing."

With blizzard conditions making it hard to see the river's edges at times, the pair finally, and carefully, arrived at the far end of the length. Their approach would be to leapfrog their way back to the top end during the day, trying all manner of spots along the way in search of a pike willing to snaffle a tasty bait.

Being familiar with the stretch you're fishing helps a lot, because you might know a few very productive spots where you can spend more time. Remember, though, that all fish in the river will

Luke Broderick

Occupation: Welder
Hometown: Dewsbury, West Yorks
Sponsors: None
Personal-best pike: 24lb 6oz

Dean Brook

Occupation: Landscape gardener
Hometown: Mirfield, West Yorks
Sponsors: Middy and 30Plus
Personal-best pike: 30lb 3oz

probably be at their lowest ebb when it's so cold, and tempting a pike under such conditions might have as much to do with good fortune as skill.

Be prepared

"It's best to set up your tackle in advance at home," explained Luke as he added a deadbait to his pre-prepared rods. "That way, you know your rigs are spot-on, and that the knots in particular are tied with warm hands. There's nothing worse than trying to handle small bits of rigs and tie knots when your fingers are numb with cold. All that's required is the bait to be mounted on the treble hooks and we'll be in business."

There is no need for anything complicated when it comes to pike rigs, however, the nature of the swims fished will dictate what kind of actual set-up will perform most efficiently.

A typical set-up on rivers like the Wharfe incorporates a sliding float. This is a useful rig because the depth of this river varies so much from one swim to another. It can be 20 feet deep in some spots and yet less than a few feet deep in others. With an easily adjustable sliding float, such variations in depth aren't a problem.

Rods for piking should be around 2.5lb test curve or above. These will enable easy casting of large, weighty deadbaits, and provide enough power to land the largest of pike! Main line should always be 15lb breaking strain or above.

Setting up the rig

1. Pass your line through a bead that has a narrow internal diameter.

2. Above the bead, tie a sliding knot made from a short piece of elastic band. The knot and elastic should be large enough so that it can't pass through the internal hole in the bead.

3. Attach your sliding pike float – an 8g Middy Pike Stem Cigar pattern is perfect. These are buoyant with a smooth rounded profile, which offers minimal resistance on the take. Luke prefers these to bung-type floats, which can make wary pike drop a bait. He uses the longer ones out in the flow, and the smaller ones down the inside.

4. Finally, add your weight attached to a clip swivel arrangement, and then a final bead to buffer against the end swivel to which is attached the wire trace. The weight keeps the bait in position and stable in the flow, and 2oz to 3oz is usually sufficient.

The rig is completed with a 24in trace of 20lb Middy Stainless Dull Black Seven Strand material, with two size 6 trebles attached at the end. Crimping down the barb or even using barbless hooks is

Tackle tip

Two size 6 trebles are attached to the middle and tail of the deadbait.

How to set up the rig

01 Thread the line through a bead and tie a sliding knot above it with an elastic band.

02 Now add your sliding pike float…

03 … then your lead arrangement.

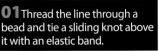

04 Finally, add a buffer bead, tie your line to a swivel and add your trace.

Tackle tip

Both anglers use 24 inches of Middy Pike System 20lb Stainless Seven Strand for their trace material.

always a good idea. All in all, it is a very basic but very effective all-round rig for piking on moving water.

The best baits

Our intrepid pikers always take along a variety of deadbaits to try, but Luke reckons a tried-and-tested few always seem to deliver the results.

"Here on the Wharfe, I have had good pike on dead rainbow trout, sprats, dead roach and dead grayling as well as 'joey' mackerel and blueys. They all work pretty well, but smelts have consistently outfished all of these baits in my experience," he said. "I don't know why smelts are best. You could argue that I have confidence in them perhaps, and use them most often of all, which would be a fair point, but when fished alongside other baits, smelts seem to attract the attention of pike first. It's remarkable how often this happens. Lampreys and eels are also high up on my list of effective deadbaits."

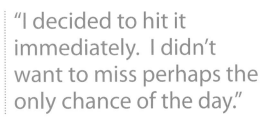

"I decided to hit it immediately. I didn't want to miss perhaps the only chance of the day."

Quite why pike will eat dead sea baits may always remain a mystery. Perhaps they just fancy something different in their diet! Dean reckoned it's simply to do with them being lazy scavengers.

"Pike have evolved into the ultimate predator. Their place in the ecosystem is essential," he explained. "Not only do they help to control populations of other fish, they also clean up a lot of dead fish. They scavenge just as much as they attack live prey, and I dare say that in the colder months they will be keener to pick up a dead fish rather than use a lot of energy chasing a live one."

Wonderful scene

Despite the cold, Luke enthusiastically mounted the baits on to the trebles and prepared to cast

At 14lb, it's not Luke Broderick's biggest-ever pike, but it's certainly one of his most satisfying.

them out as the grey, snow-filled clouds parted for a while to allow the landscape to shine under a clear blue sky above.

Swim selection on such a varied river as the Wharfe entailed a lot of sensible decision making, but inevitably there will also be some aspect of 'suck it and see'.

Dean explained: "We often leapfrog each other along the river, dropping baits into likely looking 'holes', but we are never afraid to try the not so likely looking spots too. What I mean by this, is that by dropping baits into new places you start to learn a lot more, and often surprise yourself. Possibly the biggest lesson we have learnt is just how close the pike can be found to the margins, even in winter."

Dean believed this is partly down to them trying to conceal themselves, and partly down to them holding up in slow or dead water where they don't have to expend much energy as they might have to in the main flow.

However, there are also times when the pike will be massed together in a deep pool, more than likely where the roach or dace shoals will be located too.

All in all then, it pays to not only try the most obvious spots such as overhanging trees and bushes in the water, which are natural food traps, but it also can pay dividends to experiment a fair bit with baits left down the edge or cast into those deep holes.

Keep things moving

In winter, it's more important than ever to twitch the baits after they have been in the water a short while.

"I have observed pike in clear water sit and look at a bait for ages before deciding either to take it or just disappear!" said Dean. "What I did discover, though, was that a slight twitch of the bait induced the pike to snatch at it almost instinctively. Those inducements of movement every few minutes can make the difference between success and failure in winter."

Meanwhile, time of day can often have a bearing

on when pike feed, according to Luke.

"On some waters, you can almost set your watch by pike feeding times. We have found three peak periods of the day when most of the action tends to happen. First light, last light and between 11am and 1pm tend to be the most productive times. Once again, though, there are lots of exceptions to these loose rules of thumb."

Luke's story

Today, just one pike decided to play by the rules, with Luke being the lucky angler.

"Between the blizzards and the clearer parts of the day when we had messed about a bit throwing a few snowballs at each other, waiting for the pike to find the bait, I had passed through several of my favourite reliable swims. However, significant time spent in each one had not produced even a pick-up.

"It was fun to be out in the snow, but time was pressing on. Even the usually magic time between 11am and 1pm had slid by and it looked like the cold may have subdued the pike too much!

"But I am persistent when piking, and rarely give up hope. On a river, there is always a new place to cast the bait, so eventually I dropped into a very steep-banked swim and cast one bait to the far side slack, and one was dropped down the near side.

"The near-side bait – a sardine, which always has a good blood trail when punctured – had barely been in the water a couple of minutes when I saw the line twitch and tighten and the float scudded a little across the surface. I decided to hit it immediately – it had to be a pike – and I didn't want to miss perhaps the only chance of the day.

"I called to Dean to bring the net as it felt like a decent fish. The fight was determined and fairly prolonged, and when at last the pike came to the surface I was pleased as I could see it was a 'double'.

"It made a few last-gasp thrashes at the net, but the hook-hold was firm and Dean easily scooped the fine pike into the waiting landing net, much to our obvious delight! At 14lb it wasn't my biggest pike by a long margin, but I don't go fishing to play a numbers game. I just revelled in the moment of capture and after a few pictures I slid the magnificently marked predator safely back into the cold water."

Dean added: "There's something special about a day's fishing when the world is covered with fresh white snow. When the river is at perfect trim, I always seem to do well whenever snow comes – maybe it's the low pressure? Who knows? Just being out there and catching a pike in a world of white is a wholly satisfying experience."

Tackle tip

Here's the finished rig – simplicity itself

Mad dog's and Englishmen go out in the midday... snow?

The kebab RIG

This is a completely different slant on fishing a static bait on the bottom or popped up. It was developed by top predator angler Mick Brown and has proved to be a great tactic when traditional methods fail. It can be fished on a float setup, or hard on the bottom, or popped-up on leger tactics. It's best to fish the kebab using a single large hook, or a single treble.

How to make the kebab

What you need

- 1 x predator-style stop
- 1 x small bead
- 1 x large slider-style float
- 1 x free-running weight
- 1 x buffer bead
- 1 x quick-change swivel
- 1 x large sleeve
- 1 x 20in wire trace
- 1 x size 6 semi-barbed treble hook or size 4 single hook

Select a small deadbait (a small joey mackerel is ideal).

Cut the bait up into 1in chunks with a sharp knife.

Next thread three or four chunks on to a rig pin.

How to make the rig

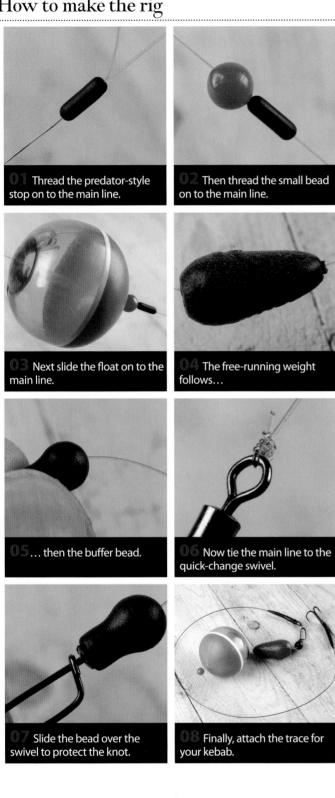

01 Thread the predator-style stop on to the main line.

02 Then thread the small bead on to the main line.

03 Next slide the float on to the main line.

04 The free-running weight follows…

05 … then the buffer bead.

06 Now tie the main line to the quick-change swivel.

07 Slide the bead over the swivel to protect the knot.

08 Finally, attach the trace for your kebab.

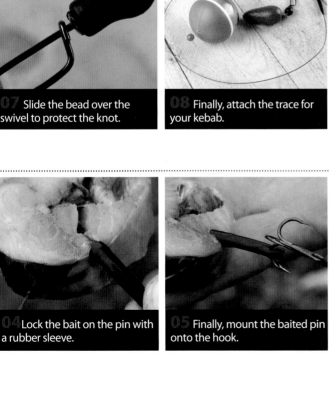

04 Lock the bait on the pin with a rubber sleeve.

05 Finally, mount the baited pin onto the hook.

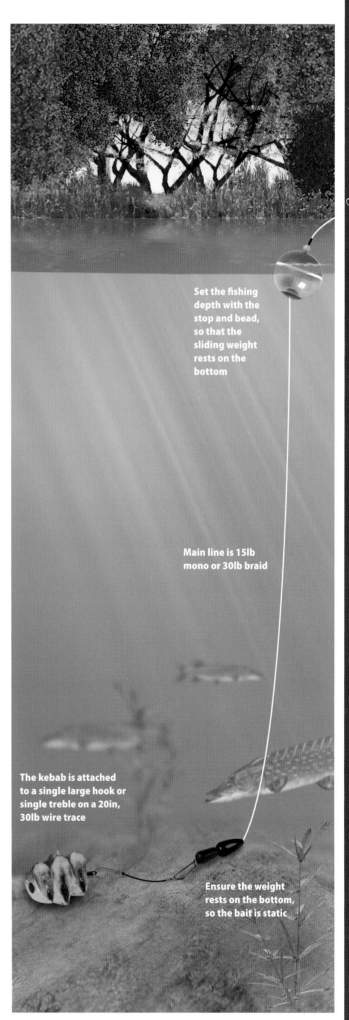

Set the fishing depth with the stop and bead, so that the sliding weight rests on the bottom

Main line is 15lb mono or 30lb braid

The kebab is attached to a single large hook or single treble on a 20in, 30lb wire trace

Ensure the weight rests on the bottom, so the bait is static

Man vs monster!

Steve Martin recalls the day he bagged his first catfish – not an experience he planned to repeat. But then...

The thought of fishing for, and catching a big, long, slimy, smelly catfish had never been top of my list of species to catch before I die, especially having seen the massive fish they catch in Spain.

However, the thought of catching an 'English' catfish started to appeal, so I felt that maybe I should make an effort to try and bag an English moggie, as it was one of the few UK species that I had yet to catch. The problem was, how did I go about it?

The opportunity

The problem for me was finding the time, as I already had a full programme with match and specialist sessions taking up most of my fishing.

The chance came thanks to a friend who had some fishing on a small Midlands lake, which I had started to fish for carp, tench and bream. He had hinted that there were other species in the water, but there is a certain stigma surrounding catfish – they're not supposed to be here at all, and many fear that once in a water they will devastate the resident population. From the sport I had been experiencing on the lake, however, this didn't ring true – well, not this time.

So, having confirmed that the catfish were in residence, it was agreed that we would target them when the conditions were favourable.

Missing moggies

My friend kept records of all the specimen fish caught on the water, and the logs of the past five years showed that there hadn't been a catfish caught in all that time. Earlier logs showed catches of small double-figure 'kittens', but these fish had not shown since, despite regular efforts to catch them.

Interestingly, those early recorded catches showed the fish had come at the end of particularly cold winters, just as the water had started to warm up. Then there seemed to be a small window when the fish fed, before they 'went missing'! And they had not showed since.

Rig essentials

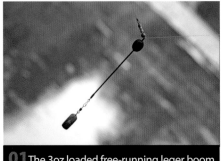

01 The 3oz loaded free-running leger boom is stopped using a soft bead and a buffer bead.

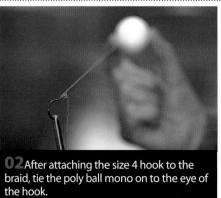

02 After attaching the size 4 hook to the braid, tie the poly ball mono on to the eye of the hook.

03 When in the water, the poly ball keeps the bait active in mid-water levels.

Could they all have died? Not according to my fishing partner, as he had seen the telltale signs from a striking fish on many occasions, but they just would not take his bait!

All the discussions about catfish took place over the winter months, and it was decided to start to target the species as soon as there was an improvement in the weather. Little did we know that we were about to endure one of the coldest winters for many years! Was the 'ice age' ever going to end?

All the gear…

You need some serious gear to fish for catfish, as they are 100 per cent muscle and, once hooked, pull back like hell! I managed to find a 3lb-test-curve rod and a large-capacity big reel – these fish are likely to strip off many metres of line when they run, and run some more, so I was told. This was loaded with 15lb mono, a safe strength, as long as there aren't too many snags. There are loads of lilies in the lake, but it's too early in the growing year for them to be a problem. For bite indication I had my trusty bite alarms and bobbins.

What bait is best?

Baits for catfish can seem a little confusing. The fish seem to eat just about anything as they scavenge the lake bed. The choice is limitless – big pellets, deadbaits, leeches, liver and even big chunks of luncheon meat. However, while in Spain, I watched the anglers from the boats fish big livebaits, which meant that the fish did not just feed on the bottom.

On my first every visit to the River Ebro, an expat asked me if I saw anything unusual about the water. It took a few minutes, but then I realised that there were no water birds anywhere on the water. It seemed that any waterfowl that did venture out into the open water were easy pickings for the monsters that lay beneath the surface.

The rig

There seem to be a number of different rigs that can be used when targeting catfish, but I wanted to keep it simple. I decided on a standard polyball rig that held the bait suspended in the water, where it fought against the buoyancy, and this movement would get the attention of any passing catfish. That was the theory, anyway!

My rig consisted a 3oz running lead, stopped by a large swivel and buffer bead. The hook link was length of heavy braid, to which I tied a size 4 hook. To give the rig its buoyancy, I attached two small polyballs to a length of 5lb mono and tied this directly on to the hook. This would quickly

Steve targeted a swim that offered plenty of shade and cover – the perfect catfish lair.

How to hook a livebait

01 Push a small piece of elastic band onto the hook, down to the bend.

02 Attach the fish by hooking it through its mouth and out the nostril.

03 Add another small piece of elastic band on to the hook for security.

break off if the fish passed through a snag. The bait was then hooked through the mouth and cast out. I was ready to try and catch my first moggie.

Muggy conditions

The temperature started to rise at the beginning of March. However, the water stayed very cold, and all we could catch were small pike. We fished at every opportunity that month, but there were so signs of a cat!

Things began to look up as April began. There was a minor spring heatwave, a regular occurrence since the turn of the century. The warm, muggy conditions on a stiff westerly breeze was perfect for catfish, so I was informed.

One-cast cat

A week into the month I received a call to say that my mate had a small-double catfish, and would I come and take the pictures. It weighed in at about 11lb – the first fish from the lake for nearly five

Steve's Tackle

01 3oz leads
02 Size 4 hooks
03 Polyballs
04 Soft beads
05 Buffer beads
06 Large swivels
07 45lb braid
08 Pieces of elastic band
09 Pop-up leger boom
10 15lb main line
11 Large Baitrunner reel
12 12ft, 3lb-test-curve rod

years. Would the others also be feeding?

A week later I finally made my first cast. Two more fish had come from a swim at the left-hand end of the dam where the wind had been continually blowing into for the past two weeks. I was told it was now or never, as the forecast indicated that the cold front was coming.

It was early evening when I arrived at the lake, and cast out to a mark close to the right-hand bank, where the water was a little deeper. My bait hadn't been in the water more than five minutes when the alarm screamed, and didn't stop until I grabbed the rod and struck hard!

Tug-of-war

You hear all the stories about how hard catfish fight, but it's not until you actually play one that you realise just how hard! As I struck, there was an almighty splash, as a massive tail broke the surface. Then, and it was a good job that I'd set the clutch, this fish tore off out into the middle of the lake. Now, I've caught 20lb carp and double-figure barbel, which can put up a good scrap, but this was something else!

The first task was to stop the fish from running, and with a lot of side strain and gritted teeth I managed it. Then it was like a game of tug-of-war until I finally started to gain line. Twenty minutes later, the fish was finally netted. I was knackered, but there was a big smile on my face. I had bagged my first catfish. It was even better than that, though. The scales registered 31lb 4oz, making it my heaviest British fish and the biggest catfish taken from the lake. What a feeling!

So, having finally caught my first catfish, would I do it again? I just might…

A first-ever catfish, and at 31lb 4oz it's a lake record for Steve – skill or luck?

Bishops Bowl Fishery

Now under the ownership of Shaun and Sarah Smart, Bishops Bowl Fishery is situated in a former limestone quarry that has been allowed to flood naturally. The site boasts a selection of lakes set within 90 acres of an attractive stone-faced bowl. This unique fishery offers a wide variety of lakes that cater for anglers of all abilities. Nestled in the Warwickshire countryside between the villages of Bishop's Itchington and Harbury, Bishops Bowl Fishery is a Site of Interest for Nature Conservation, and consists of two areas that are designated Sites of Special Scientific Interest.

PIKE AND PERCH FISHING

Two lakes: the 5-acre Mitre with pike to 28lb, and the 23-acre Greenhill (not fished for pike prior to 2010) that produced six fish over 20lb last season, plus numerous mid-doubles

Tackle and bait shop selling lures, livebaits and deadbaits

Café opening 2011/12

Pike fishing October to March only, 7am to 5pm, plus night fishing

Five other lakes for mixed coarse fishing and pleasure, club and match bookings, plus specimen carp fishing

On-site toilets

Tel: **01926 612379**

www.bishopsbowlfishery.co.uk

Bishops Bowl Fishery, Bishop's Itchington, Leamington Spa, Warwickshire CV47 2SR

Spoons & spinners

Here's a guide to the various pieces of metalwork on the market designed to catch more fish... and anglers.

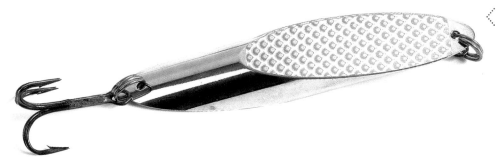

Pirk

A heavy metal lure, usually chrome-plated, with a swivel at one end and a strong treble at the other. A specialised lure in freshwater, although commonly used at sea, it's worked in a jigging fashion in deep water close to the bottom and is something you might use on trout reservoirs that allow pike fishing, loughs or lochs.

Spoon

Metal lures with a rear treble designed to be fished deep on a slow retrieve with the spoon wobbling like an injured fish. Spoons, as the name suggests, derived from actual kitchen spoons when an angler would cut the spoon from the handle, drill a hole at either end, and attach a split ring at one end and a hook at the other. Obviously they have got more sophisticated these days.

01 Kuusamo Professor: Large double-hooked spoon which has been used to great effect on trout reservoirs when fished close to the bottom.

02 Abu Atom: Very popular single treble pattern for many predatory fish. Comes in a mass of colours.

03 Blue Fox Esox: Classic spoon pattern with a red flag on the rear VMC treble, it has a wide swimming action designed for a slow retrieve. Comes in six patterns.

04 Toby: Non-symmetrical body form makes the lure flutter on retrieve, while a lifelike fish design and 3D eyes give added attraction.

Spinnerbait

These are classic single hook lures that carry a weighted head with the hook covered by a multi-coloured plastic skirt, and an offset wire carrying one or more fish-attracting blades. A single hook means it can be retrieved slowly along the bottom without snagging, which makes it ideal when predators are deep and sluggish.

Blade Spinner

These have a metal blade that revolves around a central shaft, creating a flash of colour and a fish-attracting vibration that can be felt right through the rod as it is retrieved. The shaft holds a barrel which acts as casting weight. The shape of the blade governs how far from the shaft the blade spins – a 30-degree blade spinner will fish deeper than a 60-degree one. There are more of these than you can shake a stick at, some carrying feathers on the treble.

01 Reflex Spinner: This was an extremely popular lure in the 1970s, but for some reason disappeared. However, this simple, but effective, spinner is back. Easy to cast long distances and fished with a simple retrieve, this is a lure that catches all species.

02 Mepps Aglia: Made American magazine Field and Stream's list of the top 50 lures of all time. There are several patterns, some including rubber tails or fish and others holding feathers.

03 Tasmanian Devil: A bit different, these have a double plastic blade that spins around a long central shaft. Has a good casting weight and can be retrieved, trolled or jigged.

04 Cora Z Vamp: Has a bright blade and a decent casting weight. One good feature is easily interchangeable blades.

05 Vibrax Shallow: A wide, 60-degree blade means this one fishes shallow. Vibrax blade spinners are designed to create extra underwater vibrations due to a knurling of the barrel.

The Linear pike were in a fickle mood, but Jan did manage to fool this near double-figure predator on a spinner bait.

Jan Porter

Hometown: Stratford-upon-Avon
Sponsors: Shimano, Richworth
Personal-best lure caught pike: 17lb 14oz

Venue file

Linear fisheries, Oxford.
Contact: Roy Parsons, Mobile 07885 327708
Day tickets: From £5 for one rod.
Website: www.linear-fisheries.co.uk

The big-pit alternative

Big gravel pits are not just full of specimen carp. As **Jan Porter** explains, when winter arrives, he picks up his lure rods for some rod-bending predator action.

Large day-ticket carp waters like Richworth Linear Fisheries in Oxford consist of mature gravel pits, which naturally contained pike before carp. The fact that extra pike have been stocked shows good sound business sense as well as helping to reduce the numbers of 'nuisance' fish. Small silver fish proliferate in this kind of fishery, and without control become problematic to the biomass of the main target species.

With vast shoals of roach and bream present pike help to maintain a balance as well as scavenging sick or diseased fish. So despite their savage reptilian looks and bad press they are on the anglers' side.

Apart from genuine predator hunters, big-carp anglers were the first to embrace pike angling as a natural extension to their specimen hunting/big-fish outlook. When the carp slow down for the winter the pike oblige. Without the need for too much additional kit you can fish a deadbait on almost the same kind of gear, save for a wire trace.

Day-glo displays

Lure angling has steadily built up over the last 20 years to the point that dedicated rods and more specialised tackle is now readily available. Driven by the American and Scandinavian scene, in some retail outlets it's wall-to-wall plugs, lures, spinners, spoons and rubber baits. These gorgeous iridescent and day-glo displays capture the imagination of the many 'hunter gatherers' and I'm no exception.

Rods are another item that have become more specialised and for my session I'm using a selection from the Shimano Purist range – three rods with completely different actions.

First pike

Pike may not be everybody's cup of tea, and I didn't get into lure fishing until after I turned my back on the match fishing scene in 1992. My first jack pike was taken on a chartreuse diving plug. It opened up new vista in my angling career. My

biggest lure pike – a modest 17lb 14oz critter from Barnestone in the late 1990s – was taken on a 10g spinner after letting go once before coming back for seconds. I was fishing for perch, so it was a nice bonus.

Safety first

Pike have razor sharp, hard teeth that can slice through braid and mono like a hot knife through butter, so it's important to ensure you don't cast out without first attaching a wire trace.

It's also unwise and cavalier for any novice to go out piking solo. I had the common sense to learn the ropes with experienced anglers who showed me how to handle and unhook pike to minimise damage to both parties.

An unhooking mat is a prerequisite, as is a large landing net and decent forceps or, preferably, long-nosed pliers. I always carry a set of strong wire cutters, so if I accidentally end up attached to a treble and a pike then I can snip off the hook quickly and reduce any further injury. I'd also recommend that barbs be squeezed down; okay you may lose the odd fish but this would be due to slack line rather than lack of hook-hold.

Top line TIP

Braid is the best line to use when fishing lures, as you are in direct contact with the bait, feeling every movement.

Specimen carp venues are great big-pike waters, so check out your local day-ticket pools for their predator potential.

On the move

The great thing about lure fishing is that you adopt a mobile approach, as an angler on the adjacent bank had demonstrated by catching a double and then two more pike in quick succession.

A trip around Manor Lake only produced a few follows, which got the adrenaline going, but resulted in a jack pike that wasn't much bigger than the lure. As cute as it was on a stiff jerkbait rod, it was very much a one-sided battle. It goes to show, though, that however big and daft a lure looks it won't intimidate the ferocity of an angry pike.

Having rested the St Johns swim and lacking in any real success, I returned to the peg for one

Top Hook TIP

Pinch down the barbs on the lure's treble hooks to make unhooking easier.

Match the lure to the rod

The lighter side

The 7ft/8ft Creek Critter is best described as an ultra-light spinning rod. Although it's suited for zander and perch, it will cope with bigger pike. It has a fine spliced carbon tip and is capable of casting up to 15g, which is just over ½oz in old money.
Also the softness means that when you use braid and the fish grabs hold of the lure, you don't get that sudden hard knock associated with a normal rod top.

The all-rounder

The 8ft Pikey Poker is the general all-round spinning rod in the range. It is rated to cast 15g to 40g. It's ideal for medium-sized lures and will tame fish well into double figures. It's capable of casting 1oz plugs up to 50 yards.

Top gun

With its trigger grip the 6ft 6in Little Ripper is best described as a jerkbait rod. It has the capability of whacking out 3oz (90g) lures. It's a powerful fast-taper rod that needs at least an ounce of casting weight to get the blank's compression kicking in.

more attempt to latch onto a better fish. And dispensing with the big lure, I plumped for one of my favourite lures – the spinner bait. Actually I have several lures that I've caught well on, but this normally gets me out of jail when all else fails.

Late action

Using the Pikey Poker rod, I waited for the braid to drop back signifying that the lure had hit the deck, and after a couple of quick pumps on the reel 'BANG' the rod top hooped round and the clutch started ticking away frantically. It was a decent fish, taking line as it fought.

I had hoped for a tail walk for the camera, but this pike wasn't in the mood for acrobatics.

At last, a decent fish and after a quick pose for the camera my face-saving snapper was gently returned to the water, none the worse for its experience. It soon powered away, its fantastic camouflaged back invisibly blending into the lake-bed coloration.

Final word

I've deliberately not gone into lures because this is a massive subject. All I can say is that any good tackle dealer will put you on the right path lure-wise. You'll buy loads that you like the look of and if it's any help I'd go for copper, chartreuse, fire tiger and silver as ball-park colours. The lure world is your oyster so to speak. My advice

Reel Deal
01 For lighter lure work Jan fished with a Super GTM 2500 reel loaded with 0.15mm PowerPro braid.
02 For all-round fishing it's the slightly larger Technium C5000 FC reel loaded with 0.19mm braid in green.
03 On the jig rod Jan used a Calcutta 100 multiplier reel loaded with 0.28mm PowerPro braid.

> 'BANG' the rod top hooped round and the clutch started ticking away frantically – fish on!

is to try and buy quality brands. Buy the best trace wire you can with snap-lock clips for total security.

I pike and predator fish all over the place now. It's a case of have rods will travel. There has never been a better time to have a go and provided you get expert tuition and put the fish's welfare first and foremost I think that the future of angling is much more promising. Young and old can enjoy this affordable and easy way to get on the angling ladder.

This small jack pike had a large appetite – the lure is almost as big as the fish is!

The popped-up deadbait
RIG

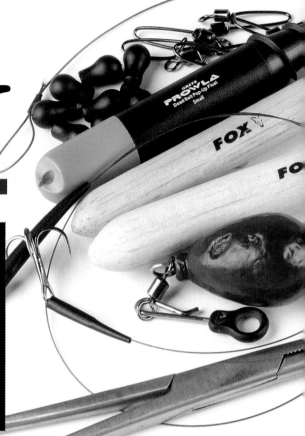

P ike, like most predators, hunt primarily by sight, especially in clear-water venues. These tend to have extremely weed-covered bottoms, so it's essential to present your bait above the cover. This rig produces a really buoyant setup that, if required, can be fished just above the bottom weed to any depth, even just below the surface. To give the bait its buoyancy, a large deadbait pencil is inserted into the bait.

What you need

1 x 3oz weight
1 x deadbait pencil
1 x buffer bead
1 x quick-change swivel
1 x run-type link swivel
1 x large swivel
2 x large sleeves
1 x length of 8lb mono
1 x 20in wire trace
1 x pop-up link
2 x size 6 semi-barbed treble hooks
1 x set of forceps

The bait stick (see inset left) creates a buoyant deadbait that sits off the bottom

The 20in trace is 30lb coated wire

Main line is 15lb mono or 30lb braid

The leger link needs to be half as long again as the trace to ensure tangle-free casting

3oz leger weight

The run-type ring is stopped above the trace with a buffer bead

How to make the rig

01 Thread a large sleeve on to a length of 8lb mono.

02 Attach the 3oz weight and slide the sleeve over the swivel.

03 Thread a second large sleeve on to the other end on the mono.

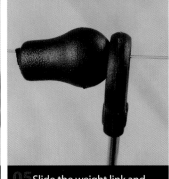

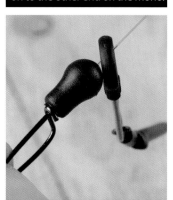

04 Now tie on the run-type swivel and slide the sleeve over it.

05 Slide the weight link and buffer bead on to the main line.

06 Tie the quick-change swivel to the main line and set the bead.

How to attach the popped-up bait

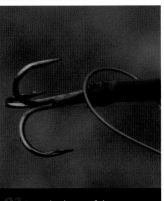

01 Pass the loop of the pop-up link over the lower treble hook.

02 Push it up the trace, and repeat for the upper treble hook.

03 Ensure the semi-frozen bait is slightly longer than the pencil.

04 Now hollow out a cavity in the bait with the forceps.

05 Push them through the bait and grip the pop-up link.

06 Pull the pop-up link back through and attach the pencil.

07 Pull the pencil back into the bait, and attach the hooks.

Sink-and-draw
secrets

With the English winter biting hard, **John Bailey** turns to one of the simplest and most overlooked piking methods: sink and draw.

Sink and draw? What am I talking about? It is simplicity itself! Basically, your line is tied to your trace and upon the two trebles you hook up a dead fish (top treble through the lips and the bottom treble in the back or flank) – preferably a roach – and cast it out. You put imagination into the retrieve to try and make the fish look as alive as possible – and that's it. Strangely, though, it's a method that is rarely used these days. If you have a copy of Pike by Fred Buller, published back in the 1970s, you will see a whole list of more complicated rigs for achieving exactly the same effect. Earlier in the 20th century, pike anglers knew the efficiency of retrieving a dead fish one way or another and they concocted all manner of spin traces to achieve different actions. I agree with the principle, but try to make the practice as simple as possible.

The tactic of sink and draw is perfect where the use of livebaits is forbidden and that is an increasing number of waters in this modern age. For me, sink and draw with a natural fish is almost always more efficient than using artificial lures. There are times when the artificial will push the natural close, but on many, if not most occasions, the natural fish will just edge ahead. And if you doubt its efficiency still, remember that the one-time English record pike of 40lb 1oz was caught by Peter Hancock using his own version of the sink-and-draw method.

Exploring the depths

What are the advantages of sink and draw then? Well, when you're using the method you keep very mobile and you are always exploring the water. This is perfect for large expanses, especially when you aren't sure where the fish are lying.

The method is also excellent for exploring any number of depths the water throws at you. If you're fishing shallow water, then you simply retrieve more quickly to keep the fish in the upper levels. If the water is deep, you let the fish sink for a longer time and retrieve it more slowly. You can put a couple of weights on the line just above the trace to achieve a deeper action. Also, in high-pressure conditions, just like we're facing today, you can work a sink-and-draw deadbait much more slowly than you can an artificial lure. This is perfect for pike that are pretty lethargic. And also, if a pike does mount an attack on days like this, it is likely to be half-hearted. They're not going to slam

John Bailey

Sponsors Hardy & Greys
Occupation Angling writer (and angler!) and tackle consultant

Mounting the bait

01 The first treble is nicked on just in front of the dorsal fin with a bait flag for added attraction.

02 The second treble, which takes all the pressure, is mounted through the top of the roach's mouth.

into a bait, but often hold it between their teeth for a while. They instantly know the difference between plastic, wood, metal and the real flesh of a once-living fish.

The weather has been bitingly cold and the water crystal clear now for three or four days. It's a wonder that the lake that we're on hasn't actually frozen over. Temperatures last night dipped down to minus 3°C and there was little wind. It's probably only the waterfowl who have kept the place ice-free for us.

> I wind down immediately, strike firmly and smoothly and the fish is on, which fights like a dervish.

My gear could not be more simple. I'm using rods of approximately nine feet – the Greys Missionary Spin range is about as good as it gets. Medium-sized fixed-spool reels, 15lb line and long wire traces. I've also set up a longer, more powerful rod to belt out a dead roach really long distances, so I can explore the distant bars and ledges. There's a healthy supply of shop-bought dead roach defrosting in the margins… but with weather this cold, it will take some time before they are nicely thawed.

Top 20

It's 9.05am. Just half an hour into the session and the fact that the roach on the end of my line is still crisp doesn't deter a beautifully conditioned mid-twenty pounder. I'm retrieving very slowly at, I guess, about 15 feet when the bait just stops. There's no pull, no tug and, for a moment, I fear I'm in weed. I immediately slacken off – this is important in case the pike feels pressure – and just a foot of line slices through the water. I wind down immediately, strike firmly and smoothly and the fish is on. It fights like a dervish – what a great start to the day. A couple of low doubles follow. In truth, they were what I was expecting – a 20lb pike will always be a bonus for any angler anywhere.

John's smile says it all as he shows off the first big 20lb-plus pike of an amazing winter-day's fishing.

Essential sink-and-draw tips

01 If you aren't careful you will miss takes using the sink-and-draw method. If a pike takes the lure and feels resistance, it will often drop it immediately. Always try to make sure that you've got some slack that you can give almost instantaneously. I'll often hold a couple of feet of line out in my left hand, especially as the bait is fluttering downwards.

02 You've got to strike pretty hard with the method. I don't know why, but you are more likely to bump a fish using sink and draw than you are when you're livebaiting. This is why it is important to keep hook points as sharp as possible. The point of the treble that goes into the fish is barbed, but I flatten down the barbs on the two free points. This makes for much easier unhooking.

03 If the pike are being really finicky, it is sometimes a good idea to have a flying treble near the head of the fish and to actually hook the bait with a single tied onto the trace with Powergum. It's not a method I resort to often, only if the fish are very picky.

Above all, strike very quickly with the method. You see far too many pike anglers giving a fish time to turn and swallow the bait and nobody wants to find themselves with a deep-hooked pike on their hands. Even if you have enough skill to get the hooks out, the stress that you will cause is enormous and must be avoided if possible.

top tip

A deadbait will slowly sink under its own weight. However, to get the bait down more quickly in very deep water, it pays to add a little extra weight to the reel line just above the trace swivel. The extra weight will also cause the bait to sink quicker rather than drift slowly downwards in shallower swims.

Short days

The winter days are so short, and before I know it the sun is already beginning to plummet towards the horizon. My breath is thick in the air and the sky is full of geese, cormorants and ducks flying in for the night. The mesh of the landing nets is frozen. There is cat ice forming on the margins, and rod rings are starting to freeze.

I was starting to think about home when, magically, I pick up another fish that I guess is about 23lb and quickly let it go to minimise the stress levels.

It has been a truly amazing day. Apart from anything else it's been just so low-tech. Could you have gear that is more simple? The only expense has been four or five packs of roach baits. There aren't any expensive lures to buy and lose with sink and draw. But above all, the method is so engrossing. It's so tactile. Most of the time you are fishing really close and you can feel and even see exactly what is going on. That is why polarising sunglasses are such an important part of your kit. There's nothing more exciting than seeing a great shape loom up behind your roach and those jaws slowly opening. Fishing is all about excitement and when you find a method

Tackle tips

01 A short, spinning-style rod, which will handle a 5in to 7in bait is ideal for John's sink-and-draw tactics.

02 A main reel line of 15lb will easily cope with fish to double the breaking strain if the fish is played carefully.

that is both thrilling and efficient, as well as economical, grab it with both hands.

The retrieve

In essence, you are trying to make your dead roach look as much like a dying fish as possible and that's where your skill and imagination come to the fore.

Twitch the fish. Let it fall motionless through the water. Give it a spurt. Leave it inert for 30 seconds. Wiggle it. Wobble it. Let it rise and fall and flutter.

In clear water, stand well back from the bank because pike will often follow the bait right into the margins before making a decision. If they see you, then it won't be the result you want. Above all, feel the line constantly and watch the rod tip. Any suspicion of a take must be investigated at once. Okay, sometimes you will get impossible-to-miss big bangs but, more often than not, you will be amazed by the subtlety even big fish can show.

Best bait

I've stressed throughout the piece that roach are my favourite deadbaits and I guess they will always remain so. It's imperative that you buy the very best you can. Pike can be very picky and roach that you don't fancy won't turn the pike on either. Ideally, I like my baits between five and seven inches long, nicely coloured and in good condition.

Once your bait begins to break up, discard it and put on a fresh one. Ideally, the roach should be totally thawed before use. Pike have an uncanny ability to sense when a bait isn't right. Also, thawed-out fish work better in the water and don't look nearly as rigid. I've not had nearly as much success with sea baits, but perhaps that's because I don't have the same levels of confidence.

Smelts have worked for me on occasions, and I always take a pack. Friends have also done well on small mackerel. These have the benefit of being tough enough to cast long range.

John returns yet another 20lb Esox back into the crystal-clear water of the magical gravel pit.

BE COMFORTABLE WITH WHO YOU ARE.

Don't follow the crowd. Check out the new Vantage clothing range. Coats, fleeces, polo shirts and hats – you name it. The protection you need on a session and the style you demand off the bank.

www.chubfishing.com   You Tube   f

VANTAGE

CHUB
SPECIALIST INNOVATION

Ten ways to catch...
pike

The UK's top predator, the pike is an aggressive hunter and can provide top action on a cold winter's day. Here are our 10 tips to help you lure the toothy critter.

Livebaits

1 These are the number-one pike baits, which are best fished on a paternoster-style rig to ensure the fish is highly visible.

Legered deadbait

2 A super distance tactic that can work well on very cold days. It's an easy option when the fish are lethargic and don't want to chase their next meal.

Float-fished deadbait

3 A great way to fish deep-water swims close in, especially on drains, slow-flowing rivers and gravel pits.

Groundbaits and flavours

4 Not a completely new idea, but one that's not often used. By feeding chunks of fish and fishy flavours in groundbait you can attract prey fish and predators with the smell.

Popped-up baits

5 These are especially deadly in venues with soft or weedy bottoms. Small polystyrene balls or balsawood inserts are best.

Wobbled deadbaits

6 An excellent method of imparting movement in a deadbait. By varying the retrieve the bait can be made to react like a wounded fish.

Find the prey fish

7 You won't find pike patrolling areas where there is no natural food, so look for signs of silver fish and read the local match reports to help with locating possible marks.

Lures

8 This is one of the most fun ways to fish for pike, as it allows you to explore a venue's many features at differing levels.

Braid or mono

9 Ten to 15lb mono is ideal for most pike fishing methods, but if you choose braid, then 30lb is the best strength to start with due to its lack of stretch. Braid is best when fishing lures to avoid tangles.

The right location

10 A pike will lie in wait for its prey to come along and then, in many cases, ambush it. Try targeting the bottom of drop-offs, boats and moorings, as well as the edge of reed beds and overhangs.

PASSIONATE A

With seven specialist titles to choose from there's a magazine for every angler, no matter what your discipline.
It's so easy to subscribe too… check out our full range of titles and pick the one that best suits you — or that special someone you're treating — and place your order.

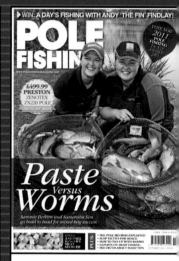

CarpFishing

Whether you've caught your first twenty or you simply want to catch much bigger fish, **Advanced Carp Fishing** is the magazine for you.

It's packed full of easy-to-read features, stunning photos and loads of top tips from the best carp anglers in the country.

www.advancedcarpfishing.com

matchfishing

Match Fishing is THE magazine to learn from. Covering all aspects of competition fishing — with in-depth features and stories from commercial fisheries and natural waters — no matter what your preference or level of ability, there is something for everyone to enjoy, every month, in Match Fishing!

www.matchfishingmagazine.com

POLE FISHING

Pole Fishing is the premier read for the angler who wants to learn more about pole fishing and the tackle used. With a team that is 100 per cent dedicated to showing you the best pole fishing tactics in an easy-to-read format, you're sure to have that red-letter day in the bag with our top advice.

www.polefishingmagazine.com

WE ARE TOO.

...BOUT FISHING?

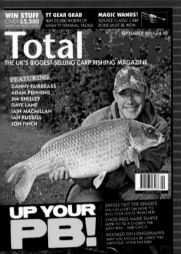

Total Carp is the fresh-faced, up-to-the-minute magazine for the modern carp angler striving for success. It's no surprise that it's also the biggest-selling carp fishing magazine in Europe. If you are new to carp fishing or simply want to improve and catch more carp, then this is the magazine for you.

www.totalcarpmagazine.com

Do you like to catch great fish from amazing venues, know all about modern techniques, keep your fishing varied and get the most from your baits? If the answers are yes, yes, yes and yes then **Total Coarse Fishing** is for you! It's an inspiring read with honest tackle reviews and will show you how to catch more quality fish.

www.tcfmagazine.com

Total FlyFisher is aimed at fly anglers with an appetite for instruction. Featuring the latest tips and techniques – as well as some of the UK's highest-profile contributors, great interviews, honest reviews and dedicated fly-tying and venue sections – it's the read no modern fly angler should be without!

www.totalflyfisher.com

Total Sea Fishing provides sea anglers with expert advice from the best anglers in the business, along with all the hottest news and gossip. You'll find no-holds-barred reviews of the latest tackle, detailed step-by-step features on how to catch the fish you seek, plus several pages dedicated to catch reports.

www.totalseamagazine.com

TO SUBSCRIBE OR FOR MORE INFO ON OUR GREAT OFFERS, VISIT:

www.davidhallpublishing.com/subscribe

or call 0845 345 0253 and quote TPFBZ11

Flesh-eating killers!

Chub will eat anything, but one of the best ways of catching them is with a juicy piece of freshly thawed fish. **Mick Brown** reveals how.

Most anglers see chub as gentle fish; going about their business quietly, feeding on any natural insect offerings that drift past their quiet lives among weed and under overhanging bushes. They are very partial to anglers' baits too, making them relatively easy to catch. There's very little we can offer them that they don't fancy. Maggots, worms and bread are all regular favourites, but they accept the modern approach with pellets and boilies just as eagerly. What few realise, though, is that the chub is a flesh-eating killer and scavenger, and even fewer use this fact to their advantage when trying to catch them!

As a predator fishing fanatic, it has been my pleasure to catch hundreds of chub on fish baits and also lures. As a teenager, I would target them with live or dead minnows and in later years with roach livebaits, mackerel deadbaits, plus a wide range of lures from spoons to plugs. Rarely have I seen anyone else do so! I've never set out to prove that this approach is always the best one, I simply enjoy seeing the chub in all its glory, as the predator it can become when it needs to.

Narrow window

When it came to making this latest feature, deputy editor Steve Martin and I scratched our heads about what to do. All the stillwaters were iced over and the rivers were in a terrible state. After some discussion, I took up the gauntlet to catch a chub from my local River Welland, which was fining down after high water. What's more, I said that I would catch one on deadbait, much to Steve's surprise!

With the river being icy cold, it was clear that chub would be the only fish that I could bank on catching. However, I knew that it would still be a challenge because the river had started to colour up and rise yet again. There was going to be a very narrow window of opportunity to get one; I was up for it, though!

I would have liked a nice deep slack, but the middle Welland isn't that sort of river, so I settled for a steady glide with just the tips of the summer bulrushes giving themselves away as they dithered in the flow. The Welland doesn't normally have much natural flow, but there was no lack of it today!

Mixed menu

I had a variety of deadbaits with me to try. I would cut them into sections, starting with very tiny pieces and trying bigger pieces up to an inch long later. I can't think of a type of deadbait that I haven't caught chub on, so I had a variety of samples. On a normal day I would have one or two different baits with me but on this session, for illustration purposes, I had herring, mackerel, smelt, sandeel and lamprey.

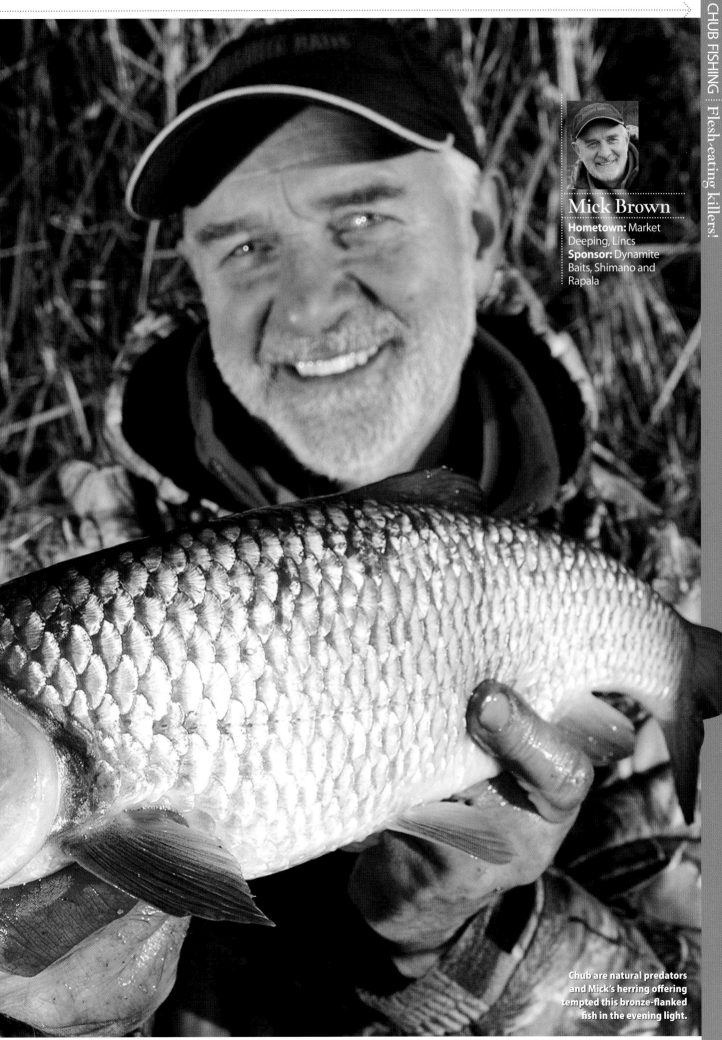

Mick Brown

Hometown: Market Deeping, Lincs
Sponsor: Dynamite Baits, Shimano and Rapala

Chub are natural predators and Mick's herring offering tempted this bronze-flanked fish in the evening light.

Location is key when targeting chub. Look for dead marginal reed beds when there are few mid-water features.

Smelly red feed

Under normal circumstances, I would fish blindly by casting a bait into a likely looking chub swim, but the increased flow and coloured water didn't make the swims too obvious. For this reason I decided to feed groundbait to try and bring chub upstream to my bait. My groundbait mix was simply a bag of Dynamite Red Crumb — a good general-purpose groundbait that I use more as a carrier and feeding stimulator than a feed. Just to make it really attractive to predators I added a small amount of Dynamite liquid fish attractor. Be warned, it has a really strong pong!

As I had decided to start with a small piece of sandeel on the hook, I cut up another couple of sandeels into very tiny pieces and mixed them in with the groundbait. All the juices from the sandeel bag were also poured into the mix, which had been made very sloppy so that it dispersed in the flow easily.

Simple setup

My tackle and rig was exactly as I would use when fishing conventionally, so that I could quite easily chop and change between 'normal' baits

As I struck, within a few seconds the telltale black tip of a chub's tail showed in the shallow water.

and fish baits, if I so wished. I used a 1lb-test-curve specialist quivertip rod and a fixed-spool reel loaded with 5lb mono. Using the popular four-turn water knot, I added a 6in dropper above an 18in hooklength — both being made from the main-line mono. I started on a size 10 hook, as I was going to start with a small bait, but if the chub start to feed quite boldly I would often go up to an 8 or even a 6. To the dropper I added two SSG weights, and to prevent them from sliding off too easily I created a knot with a simple loop.

Feed lightly

I tried to gauge where a chub might be sheltering in the flow and cast a good way downstream, putting the rod in the rest. Some time before casting out, I had already spent a while feeding the swim with small but regular balls of my smelly groundbait, laced with tiny chunks of fish. I did

a large tag, it collects small pieces of weed before they slide down your line and mask the bait.

That's no chub!

As I was beginning to think that I would have to abandon the swim, a couple of telltale knocks – quite uncharacteristic of a chub bite – saw me strike into what was obviously a fish. Feeling very smug that I had cracked it, I guided the hard-fighting fish up towards the net, only to find that it carried on running upstream against the flow. Something didn't seem right. Then it jumped out of the water, giving itself away as a lovely, well-conditioned brown trout of a couple of pounds. Not the fish that I was after, but nevertheless just as interesting. Trout, like chub, are another part-time predator with very similar habits.

I just didn't feel that it was working in the swim and, rather than flog it all day, I decided to move downstream to see if any chub had picked up the scent of my bait, which must have reached that far in the strong flow. Another hour passed and nothing happened, so I knew that it would be best to move well downstream and well ahead of the new surge of water.

Swim switch

The water a couple of miles downstream was slightly coloured from the last flood, but it hadn't received the latest deluge. With two hours of daylight remaining I baited a likely looking steady glide that, although only two feet deep, had dense vegetation along both banks, where chub would find plenty of cover in between feeding spells. I baited the swim in a similar manner but this time I mixed a fresh batch of groundbait with the juice from a bag of Dynamite herrings. Running out of time, I decided to use small pieces of herring in the mix and a chunk of about an inch long on the hook. Having caught chub accidentally when pike fishing using 6in chunks of half mackerel, to use a bait of this size didn't seem at all unreasonable.

so sparingly, though, until I had gained some idea of the chub's reaction because I didn't want to overfeed them.

An hour passed and I knew that it was going to be one of those days when my line was constantly being knocked by small pieces of weed coming down with the current. It had also become increasingly clear that the river had started to rise again. Incidentally, a useful tip is that if you leave the connecting four-turn water knot with quite

Mick's fish bait tip

Mick recommends that you take a selection of sea-fish deadbaits so that you can chop and change to find the right recipe to tempt chub on the day.

Mick's mix

01 A red breadcrumb feed is used more as a carrier than an attractor.

02 To give a strong fishy smell, Dynamite Killer Fish liquid is added.

03 The best way to blend this in is with a bankstick or large twig.

04 To give the feed an extra boost, Mick adds small pieces of fish.

05 To kick-start each swim, Mick lobs in a small ball sporadically.

Keep watching

The steadier flow made it more predictable regarding where my groundbait would be travelling, and easier to position my hook bait to take full advantage. Nothing happened for an hour, but by constantly scanning the swim I was sure I saw giveaway swirls in the current that, to my mind, were feeding chub. Whether my feed had stimulated them or whether they were feeding naturally, I couldn't say. You can never be sure of the nature of any swim. Sometimes chub will take up preferred feeding positions, but you can easily miss them and find that your bait is lying among an area of weed or silt, which they don't favour. I rather fancied that there were chub in the swim, but the lack of bites suggested that my bait was in the wrong spot. This was reinforced when I spotted potential chub swirls nearer to the far bank.

The witching hour

Time was moving fast but I was still optimistic and all fired up because the last hour of daylight in winter can often be the very best time to fish for chub. So I wasn't surprised when the tip started to move. It gave two gentle taps and a steady pull,

The business end

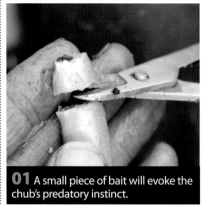

01 A small piece of bait will evoke the chub's predatory instinct.

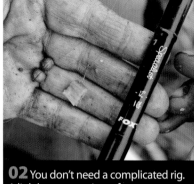

02 You don't need a complicated rig. A link-leger setup is perfect.

which brought the tip round an inch or so. As I struck, within a few seconds the black tip of a chub's tail showed in the shallow water, and I knew that I was so close to accomplishing my challenge. When netting a special fish you must concentrate fully on getting it into the net before punching the air in jubilation. So many times I have seen an angler celebrating before the fish is in the net, only to find it drops off at the last second. Indeed, it has happened to me once or twice.

Gently does it

As the fish approached the net, I could see the size 10 hook was barely holding in the lip, and the piece of herring was still flapping about on the line. It was a modest-sized chub of just a couple of pounds. At that moment it meant the world to me to get it into the net and conclude a day that had pushed me hard, not so much physically, but mentally. If it dropped off, then it was likely that the day had been wasted. Thankfully it didn't. As I dragged the net and fish back over the dense, decaying winter vegetation, and water very close to the top of my wellies, I felt that warm glow that only comes with a special fish in the net. Steve was more than happy and while he was making the long drive home, like a fool I stayed for an hour into darkness, which is often well worth the effort. I phoned Steve the next morning to tell him what he had missed — nothing! I still went home feeling very pleased with myself, though.

The first action of the day came when this brown trout homed in on Mick's sandeel portion.

Get Hooked on Fishing...

Building Positive Futures

All coaches are UKCC qualified and disclosure checked

GHOF BTEC classroom session

Peer Mentoring

WHAT DO WE DO ?

We work with local communities to help create opportunities for young people.

We deliver fun and interactive training around the sport of angling. Our programme is especially designed with the help of young people to give the participants more confidence and to demonstrate that there are alternative pathways and better opportunities available to them.

We help to train and develop peer mentors at the same time as encouraging young people to take an active part in how we run the local schemes.

We are happy to work with all young people aged 6 and over and have a proven track-record in delivering social inclusion, improvements in school attendance and educational achievement.

Learning about sharks !

" **Most Youth Service professionals who have encountered the Get Hooked on Fishing scheme have sensed something special about the project. There is an apparent synergy of vision, commitment, process and tangible outcomes.** "

(Home Office - Positive Futures) substance.

HOW YOU CAN HELP US...

"As a registered Charity, Get Hooked on Fishing relies on donations to carry out it's work. In 2010 we helped over 5500 young people through our intervention programmes - we hope to do more in 2011. Any help you can give would be greatly appreciated, so why not go online now and make a donation - help us to help them."

Get Hooked on Fishing- they both did !

so help us to help them at :

www.ghof.org.uk

LOTTERY FUNDED

Get Hooked on Fishing

Shallow & deep divers

A look at some of the bright and beautiful plugs you can buy, and what they will do to catch you more fish.

Savage Gear 4Play Swim & Jerk

This slow-sinking lure looks like the real thing when it is slowly retrieved through the upper levels. It comes in two sizes – 13cm/21g and 19cm/52g – so it requires a pokey rod to cast one.

Abu Hi-Lo

Famous floating wooden predator lures, the thing anglers love about these is that the angle of the vein can be altered from almost horizontal to nearly 90 degrees, so the depth at which these classic plugs are fished can be varied.

Cora Z Rivalo

Pike will happily eat their own kind and pike-patterned lures have become all the rage in recent years. This realistic floating plug from the Cormoran stable has a vein at about 30 degrees to the horizontal and will work at about 10 feet deep. It comes in four patterns, all resembling pike with large eyes.

WSB Tackle Jointed Plug

This is a floating, jointed lure that has an exaggerated action, which can trigger finicky fish into an aggresive take. A short downward pointing vein sees this lure working at three to six feet. Comes in two patterns and sizes.

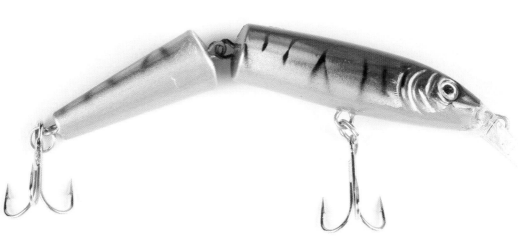

Rapala Magnum Divebait

The long, straight vein tells you that this is a lure that dives deeply when cranked in – up to 30 feet in this case. This particular lure floats, but is ideal for trolling behind a boat on large stillwaters at depths from 15 to 25 feet. Comes in 10 patterns.

Rapala Super Countdown Shad Rap

Perhaps the classic plug pattern of all time, the Shad Rap works brilliantly in fresh and saltwater. Available as a floating lure in a multitude of patterns, the Countdown is a sinking version with the vein at a sharp angle, allowing you to count the lure down to the required depth and keep it at that level on the retrieve.

Predator Q&A

Total Predator Fishing answers those nagging predator queries.

Q Can you target chub with lures?

A Although chub will take a small, shallow-diving, plug-type lure, the best and most exciting way to fire the predatory instincts of the fish is to use a surface lure under overhanging trees and tight to weeds.

Chub that live close to these features will investigate anything that drops into the water to see if it's edible, so a small, floating, insect-like lure that can be made to act like a grasshopper or caterpillar struggling in the surface tension of the water can be deadly, especially in the warmer months.

Lure fishing for chub is not that popular in the UK, but if you fancy a change from the usual float or feeder fishing tactics try lures such as Crazy Crawlers and Creek Hoppers.

Q When fishing a paternoster setup, is the length of the hook trace shorter or longer than the trace holding the weight?

A A paternoster setup tethers a live or deadbait above the bottom, so that it is very visible and doesn't drift away. It is usually set up with a 'sunk' float whose buoyancy keeps the rig in tension, preventing tangling.

It consists of a hook trace connected to a wire uptrace, which is there to prevent bite-offs if the bait should tangle with the main line. At a pivot point between the hook trace and uptrace is a link to a weight, which is normally about 1½oz to 2oz. It is this that keeps the rig from drifting away and tethers it to the bottom.

The length of this link has to be longer than the hook trace or else the bait will just drag on the bottom, defeating the point of this rig. A typical hook trace for paternostering is about 13 inches long, so the weight link needs to be at least this length. In practice, about 20 to 24 inches is about right for most situations but you can always make it a bit longer to get the bait above weed or other snags.

Q What are the best colour patterns for lures?

A There are hundreds of lures of every conceivable shape and size available, including many in the United States, which are successfully used for targeting bass. Many of them are highlighted on these pages.

However, our experts have put their heads together and come up with some styles that they say should be in every predator angler's box.

Any fish-patterned lure is well worth having, as modern ones look extremely natural and lifelike with the most successful patterns being the perch and pike.

Again on a modern theme, there are a lot of holographic styles that glint in clear-water venues and resemble a silver fish catching the light as it swims.

Two of the most popular patterns in the UK are the Red Head, a pearl or white lure with a large red patch on its head, and the Fire Tiger, a lure that has a green and yellow body with black stripes. Our experts also highlight the fact that blue and black lures, although not a popular choice, are also deadly colours, especially in coloured water and at night. Remember that a predator is usually looking up at your lure, so the stronger the silhouette it creates against the skyline the better.

The sunk-style float locks over the top swivel of the trace

The bottom of the trace features a helicopter-style setup

Hook the livebait so that it swims away from the rig

Weakened leger link

Use at least a 3oz weight for this rig

To catch a
specimen
eel

Southern big-fish expert **Duncan Charman** explains the
rules of engagement when specimen eels are the challenge.

A lthough I'm not obsessed like many serious eel anglers, I do have a passion for catching big eels that has spanned more than two decades. Every summer you will find me on a new water, looking for an eel gold mine, something that's getting rarer by the day.

Location, location

Roughly 95 per cent of stillwaters contain eels, so never ignore a water with no past record for the species; lots of monster eels come from such waters and rarely get caught, due to their feeding habits and preference for natural baits such as worms and maggots. These baits are used less these days, mainly due to the cost and the use of more convenient baits such as pellets and boilies.

Now and again one makes a mistake and gets caught by an angler targeting carp, and once the news is out the first eel angler who descends on the venue will often have numerous red-letter nights before the eels wise up.

Although most venues with an inlet or outlet will contain eels, don't ignore those without, as I have known some of the best eel waters to be in the middle of nowhere, miles from any flowing water, and certainly with no easy access. However, eels do get in by crossing land on wet nights, then they become landlocked and slowly grow big in an unmolested environment. Also, never dismiss running water, as one of my biggest-ever eels – 6lb 9oz – came from a deep, slow section of a river!

Local tackle shops and clubs will readily pass on information on this species, but remember that a 3lb eel looks massive and anglers unfamiliar with eels will exaggerate its size quite considerably.

The internet is also a great area to discover an eel gold mine. I recently discovered such a venue by seeing a young angler on a day-ticket water's online picture gallery. More of the session on this water later, although even though I was there it wasn't me who reaped the benefits.

Duncan Charman

Hometown: Aldershot
Sponsor: Korum and Sonubaits

Duncan's top-five eel tips

01 Remove your lead and replace with a link leger if you're missing bites.

02 Prawns are a great bait for eels and will help hook bites that are missed on worm.

03 PVA bags of maggots soaked in a flavour additive will add attractant to your hook bait.

04 Reduce resistance from a taking fish by pointing your rod directly where you cast it.

05 Light bobbins on a long drop can work if runs are being dropped.

If big eels are the target, then fish into the darkness when the fish are at their most active.

Two-pronged tactics

Eels are predominantly nocturnal, rarely feeding during daylight, and the first night on a new water would see me taking two approaches. The first rod would be baited with two lobworms and fished over a bed of dead maggots, normally fished in the margins to avoid nuisance fish. The second rod would have a small deadbait – either the head or tail of a rudd, if possible – fished on a J S Eel rig and cast further out into open water.

Eels have an incredible sense of smell and will find your bait easily from a great distance. I would never place these two rods in close proximity to each other, and would expect enquiries to both rods on that first night, even if eels don't show – normally pike to the deadbaits (although on occasions carp, bream and even barbel), and most species to the worms. If one area continued to produce runs from eels while the other rod remained motionless then I would reposition the quiet rod, so it fished nearby, but this would be the only time I would fish both in the same area.

Monkey climber

Eels are similar to perch and zander, and will not tolerate resistance, so one of the most important parts of eel fishing is to find an indicator setup that is not only visual, but which also allows line to be taken on the free spool in the event of a take. The method I use is to pull the line into a clip that is tied to the rod rest below the reel. Although the line is tight, the slightest pull will release the clip and allow line to be taken.

Unfortunately, fishing a free spool has its

A calming influence

01 Place your eel on a mat and turn it over.

02 After a few attempts you will be able to leave it in this position.

03 If you look closely at the head, notice the gills filling with air.

04 The becalmed fish is now ready for that all-important trophy shot.

disadvantages, as line can pass over some makes of electronic indicator without turning the wheel, giving no audible indication apart from a single bleep as the clip is released. It's important to stay vigilant and alert to any single bleeps. Even better, and something that I have started using, is the years' old 'monkey-climber' system, as this will alert you to a run when the indicator rises, then line is taken once it's tipped over.

Danger baits

If I notice a trend forming where the eels show a preference to a certain bait (and they will), then it's time to change both rods over, so they are fishing the same bait. Eels do have a bait preference on each water, so you need to maximise your chances as quickly as possible. Believe me, if you think you will continue to catch on this bait forever and a day, then you are mistaken. Make the most of the bait that's catching because runs will eventually dry up, and after a few captures it will be time for a change, but to what?

Eels will soon associate a bait with danger; how they do this is a mystery, but runs will start to dry up. This is the time to experiment with other baits, as they will start feeding differently. I remember one spring catching 11 5lb-plus eels from a water in one month. The first few fell to worms, and when bites dried up I caught on small deadbaits before the last one came to a small live perch. After this it was as if the lake contained no eels at all!

Rare creatures

While small eels seem to hang themselves, big eels can be extremely difficult to hook and are a completely different prospect. The big specimens will only venture out and feed on nights when the oxygen levels, water temperature and atmospheric conditions are favourable. They will often go on a feeding frenzy during this time, only then to become completely inactive for long periods, similar to catfish. If you do venture on to a new water, remember that timing is of the essence. Even after numerous blanks, you may still be on an eel goldmine without knowing it.

To catch a big eel by design often takes many hours of dedication, persistence and, at times, sheer frustration, but the capture of a specimen eel in excess of 4lb has to be remembered and cherished, as they are becoming rarer each and every year.

Handle with care

For the inexperienced angler, handling an eel of any size becomes a real nightmare. As with many species, however, the larger the specimen gets, the easier it is to control. Large eels of over 4lb are probably the easiest of fish to handle if you follow a few easy steps.

Once landed, remove the eel from your landing net as soon as possible and move it to a wetted mat. Do not try and remove the hook immediately.

Gently turn the eel onto its back and run your fingers down its belly a few times. Each time this is done you will notice the eel slowly calming down, and after a few strokes the eel will go into a state of paralysis. It is believed that the eel goes into this state because it cannot draw oxygen through its gill covers and so goes into a trance, protecting itself, but the real reason isn't known. It is important that the eel is only kept in this position for the shortest period possible – left like this the consequences could be fatal!

Hopefully the hook (barbless please – don't use barbed hooks when eel fishing unless the rules state otherwise) will be in sight and, once the eel has become immobilised, a pair of forceps (or large disgorger, if deep-hooked) will release the hook easily. However, the vital organs are found just inside its mouth, so don't go prodding around too much.

Action in the dark

Now, back to that water I discovered on the web. I decided to try my luck with a friend who was keen to up his personal best, which stood at 2lb 7oz. With no idea what to expect we set up to fish late into the evening, and overnight. As it turned out, we had a sleepless night, as the conditions were perfect for eels.

My fishing partner had five big eels after dark, including a brace of 4lb fish, all coming to small fish sections. I had countless runs from small fish, but on this occasion failed to bag a real specimen to match the last big eel I had, which weighed in at 5lb 13oz. As you might guess, it won't be long before I return for another try.

Follow Duncan's advice and you could bag a monster eel like this 5lb 13oz specimen.

The J S Eel Rig

Duncan recommends this rig for all your eel sessions. "Why this rig is so effective I don't know, but I use it for 90 per cent of my eel fishing and suffer very few dropped runs," he explains.
The rig comprises a 1½oz gripper lead that has had the swivel removed and a Korum Running Clip added to reduce resistance. A Korum buffer bead then protects a large swivel, as well as buffeting the lead. Fifteen inches of main line is then attached to this before tying on another swivel. To this, 12 inches of Kryston 25lb Quicksilver is added before the rig is finished with a size 6 Korum S3 barbless hook. A sliver of elastic band is added to lock the hook bait in place.

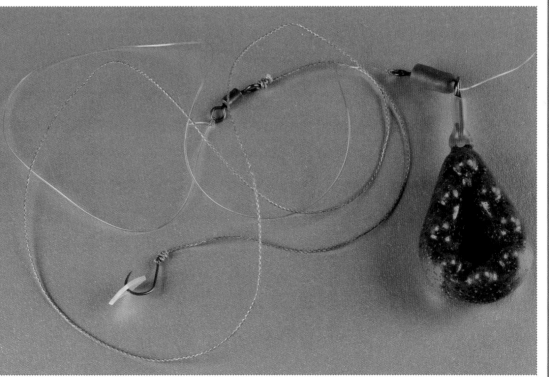

The best perch rig ever...
...and here it is!

Top specialist **Neil Wayte** reveals the rig that's seen him catch some outstanding specimen perch from big southern stillwaters.

Neil Wayte
Sponsor: Gardner Tackle

Britain's ever-increasing demand for carp fisheries has seen countless gravel pits stocked with more and more of this popular species. This is great for carp anglers, and great for those who prefer other species too!

Why? Well, because of this single-species preoccupation, the many other inhabitants tend to be left alone. Perch fall into this category and there are literally thousands of gravel pits waiting to be exploited.

For this session I'm fishing at Westhampnett gravel pit, near Chichester in West Sussex. CEMEX Angling runs the fishery primarily as a carp syndicate, but it has a fantastic head of other species as well. I first became aware of the perch in the pit when the head bailiff told me about some of the fish that he had caught when the carp fishing was a bit slow. No-one had really targeted them seriously.

The hardest job

With waters as big as this one – more than 40 acres – locating perch is the hardest job. Fortunately, gravel pits tend to have gin-clear water, so time spent walking around carefully watching the margins will pay dividends. Small groups of fish can often be seen patrolling the bottom of the marginal shelf, constantly on the move hunting for food. Now, because we can't see what's going on out in the pit, this is where I start to target them.

The choice of bait is very simple: lobworms and

Rig tip
The swivel at the top of the hooklength can rotate between the two beads but the float stops keep everything secure on the cast.

red maggots. However, subtle changes to how these are used can give you an extra little edge.

My rods are light-test-curve Avon-style and these carry small Baitrunner-type reels loaded with 8lb main line. This might seem on the heavy side, but there is always the possibility of picking up a large carp, bream or tench, and line of 8lb breaking strain gives me the chance of landing these bonus fish.

My rig for perch

The rigs that I use go totally against the commonly accepted theory that if perch feel resistance they tend to drop baits. My favourite rig for fishing lobworms is a fixed paternoster that incorporates a blockend swimfeeder on the bottom rather than a leger weight.

Here's how to make my simple, but brilliant, rig:
Step 01: First, feed a rubber float stop onto the line. Those sold as braid stops are my favourite because they grip 8lb main line tightly and do not slip when casting.
Step 02: Thread a small rubber bead, around 4mm, on to the line.
Step 03: Now add a size 12 swivel.
Step 04: Next, thread on another 4mm bead.
Step 05: Feed a second float stop on to the line.
Step 06: Tie your blockend feeder on to the end of the line.
Step 07: Finally, slide an anti-tangle sleeve on to a 6in hooklength and tie this to the swivel. The final anti-tangle sleeve on the hooklength helps to keep the

Neil prefers to use three rods, allowing him to explore different areas. Make sure your bobbins are heavy enough to counter tow.

At 2lb 14oz, this is typical of the size of perch to be found in many gravel pits.

hook bait away from the main line when casting to prevent it tangling.

Even if you push the float stops together, the swivel can still rotate around the main line, but the setup remains together during casting.

However, you will find that the bottom float stop and bead will be pushed down towards the feeder when a fish is hooked. Because the components are all soft, there is no chance of damaging the main line. Plus, you have the added advantage that it is possible to move them up and down the main line so that you can change the distance that you fish the bait above the feeder.

This can be important if there was weed on the bottom of the pit and the lobworms are being pulled into it by the weight of the feeder. By increasing the distance between the beads holding the swivel and the feeder, you can perfect everything so that the lobworm comes to rest on top of the weed and is still visible. This is important because perch are predominately sight feeders.

Hooklengths are either 4lb or 6lb fluorocarbon, depending on how weedy the swim is, and the hook is usually a size 10 wide-gape Gardner Talon Tip. I prefer a wide gape when using lobworms because the point stands clear of the bait, even when a big, juicy bait is used.

A red maggot or two is also used with the lobworm hook bait to add a bit of colour.

It is worth pointing out that a free-running feeder setup would create less resistance to a taking perch, but I have found that this type of setup can lead to perch being deep-hooked. Every perch is lip-hooked with the paternoster rig that I have described. However, it is important not to use a long

hooklength with this setup because you will end up with the same problem of deep-hooking.

My standard setup now is a hooklength of no more than six inches, set so that the distance between the beads holding the swivel is also six inches above the feeder, unless the swim is weedy.

Three-rod approach

Gravel pits can be huge and I like to cover as much water as possible by using three rods. This allows me to space my hook baits out along the bottom of the marginal shelf and slightly vary the distance from the bank at which I place my baits.

> Takes can be aggressive and short hook links are imperative to prevent deep-hooked fish.

In clear water it is often possible to see the bottom of the shelf, so one bait is cast there. The next two are cast slightly further out so that if the fish are not following the very bottom of the shelf as they wander around the pit, it is still possible to pick them up.

By recasting every 30 minutes or so you build up the amount of bait over each area. I'm sure that the maggots coming out of the feeder as it falls attracts the perch into the swim. It also pays to regularly catapult a few maggots around each bait to keep a trickle of bait falling through the water.

The small canal-type match catapults are great for this because they only hold a few maggots and stop you from going mad with this extra feeding.

Bait tricks

I hook a lobworm through the saddle and tip it off with a red maggot. This catches plenty of perch but, if things are going slowly, I switch to half a lobworm. By using a broken worm you give the perch a smaller bait, but the leaking juices are an extra attractant.

Although all predators are sight feeders by nature, they also scent their prey. So by using just half a worm you can use this to your advantage. Another great tip is to use a small syringe to inject air into the worm. Insert the needle into one end and inject just a small amount of air. Now drop the worm into the margins to see how it floats. You are looking to get just one end of the worm floating up off the bottom to attract to any wandering perch. Take great care when using syringes and needles, though, because they are dangerous.

Pep up your feeder mix

01 Drop a few maggots and a couple of lobworms in a small tub.

02 Chop everything up with a large pair of scissors.

03 Now squirt a little worm liquid into the mix. Not too much or it will go everywhere!

04 Pour it into the feeder, pop the cap on, and cast quickly.

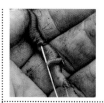

Perch tip

Carefully inject air into the worm to give a buoyant bait that sits above the bottom weed.

By injecting more air and making the worm completely buoyant, this method can also be used to make the worm float up completely off the bottom or over weed. The takes on this method can be aggressive and short hook links are imperative to prevent deep-hooked fish.

Add an extra edge

On the subject of scents, match anglers have been using chopped lobworms as a method of attracting fish into their swims in winter for years.

Now it's a silly specimen angler who doesn't take notice of what other branches of the sport are doing when targeting the same species, especially in what are less-than-favourable conditions. I stated earlier that I recast every 30 minutes or so to keep a trickle of fresh bait going into the swim, but in colder conditions, like today, every third cast I fill the feeder with a mix of chopped lobworms, chopped maggots and worm liquid that's popular with match anglers.

It's not the nicest-smelling concoction and it is messy to make, but I'm sure that it increases my catch rate. All the worms and maggots are put in a small pot and then cut up. When I have just small chopped maggots and worms left I then add a small amount of worm liquid. This is then poured into the feeder and cast out. Don't go mad with the amount of liquid because it will run out of the holes in the feeder before you can recast.

Bite detection

For bite detection I use buzzers and bobbins. The size of the bobbins is kept to a minimum but because of the underwater tow on these big pits I carry three different weights so that I don't have the problem of the bobbin being pulled up tight all the time as the tow pulls the line.

For this session I used a rod pod because the ground was so hard, and set the bobbins right down at the bottom of the length of the chain.

If perch are in the area it won't be long before you get a take. However, if nothing has happened after a couple of hours, be positive and move. With a cold northerly wind, I moved to a spot where the wind wasn't hitting the water. Grebes had been working this shoreline close to the bushes so it was a pretty safe bet that there were silver fish in the area. With any luck, the perch wouldn't be far behind.

An hour after moving I was beginning to wonder if I was going to catch, but in typical perch fashion I received a short but hectic flurry of action as a small shoal of fish moved through the swim. Unfortunately, the first fish broke the hook link, something that seems to happen only when you are struggling for a bite!

I was retying the link when the left-hand rod signalled a bite and bad luck struck again when the hook pulled during the fight.

This felt like a really good fish but I think I hit the bite too soon in my eagerness to catch. Thankfully, the remaining rod signalled a bite almost immediately. This is typical of the action you receive when a shoal of perch moves into your swim.

This fish weighed 2lb 14oz; typical of the size that I've been catching this winter. There are bigger fish here but the shoal fish that I've been catching all seem to be around this size. Just to prove the case, a few minutes after rebaiting all the rods, another bite produced a fish of 2lb 12oz. It was a cracking brace of fish after a slow day, but very welcome in the bitterly cold conditions.

Perch are sight feeders, and as you can see from this image, the hook bait and feed are highly visible in the clear gravel-pit water.

MADE IN THE UK

NEW
BUG WEIGHTS

COLOUR RANGE

BUG CRADLE

NEW

SIZES AVAILABLE

GET THE BUG
GET THE BITE

GARDNER
www.gardnertackle.co.uk

just add carp!

The stuff you need for...
lure fishing

Here's a list of the essentials you'll need for a day's lure-fishing fun...

01 Unhooking tools
Lure hooks tend to be a thicker gauge, so take some extra-long needle-nosed pliers and a set of long side cutters, just in case…

02 Traces
Make sure you carry a supply of different-strength lure traces to cover different venues.

03 Polarising glasses
These are an essential requirement to enable you to look beneath the surface for any fish following the bait as you retrieve it.

04 Spare jig heads
When fishing jelly lures you can change the casting weight and hook size depending on the size of jig head you fit.

05 Braided lines
The most popular strength for general lure tactics is 30lb test, but if big lures are your thing use 60lb test to help you pull free of snags.

06 Split-ring pliers
This is a must-have tool if you want to replace a set of blunt treble hooks quickly on the bank.

07 Hook sharpener
Don't let your favourite lure let you down with blunt hooks. Check and sharpen the points regularly.

08 Rods
Ensure you choose the right rod for the size of lure you want to fish.

09 Lure selection
Predators will patrol any depth so, before you set off on your trip, pack a selection of baits to cover from the surface to the deck.

10 Reels
Baitcaster or fixed-spool reels can be used to fish lures.

The wobbled-deadbait RIG

PREDATOR CARBO FLEX
7 STRAND CARBON C
STAINLESS STEEL L
30lb 15m
FOX

This is a very popular method to fish a deadbait on venues, rivers and stillwaters where livebaiting is not permitted. The bait is cast out and allowed to sink to the bottom, and then is retrieved in a way that makes it act like a wounded or dying fish. The rig explained here includes the addition of beads and a small spinner blade, which gives extra visible attraction as the bait is retrieved.

What you need

- 2 x size 4 treble hooks
- 3 x crimps
- 2 x long sleeves
- 1 x treble sleeve
- 1 x large swivel
- 1 x bait flag
- 1 x length of 30lb trace wire
- 3 x small beads
- 1 x spinner blade
- 1 x crimping pliers

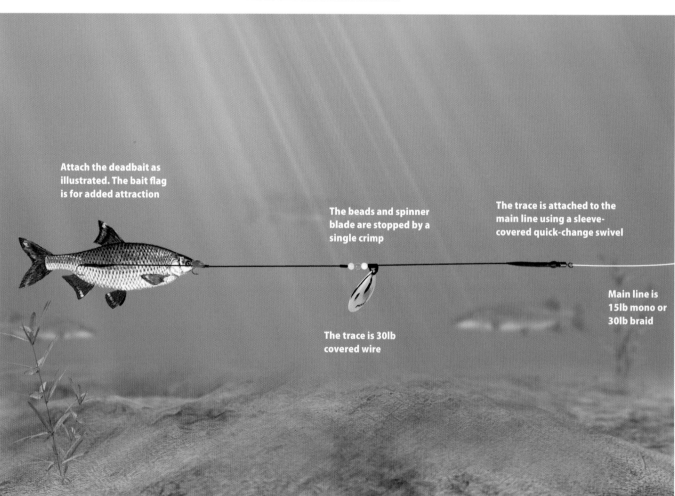

Attach the deadbait as illustrated. The bait flag is for added attraction

The beads and spinner blade are stopped by a single crimp

The trace is attached to the main line using a sleeve-covered quick-change swivel

The trace is 30lb covered wire

Main line is 15lb mono or 30lb braid

How to make the trace

01 Firmly attach the bottom treble to the trace wire using a crimp and pliers.

02 Slide a long sleeve down the wire and over the crimp and hook shank.

03 Fix the second treble hook approximately four inches from the first.

04 Slide the treble sleeve down the wire and over the shank of the second hook.

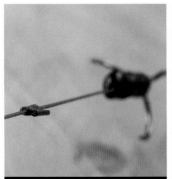

05 Attach a crimp about three inches from the second treble hook.

06 Thread the three beads and the spinner blade on to the wire, down to the crimp.

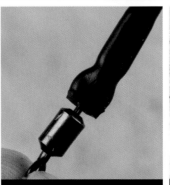

07 Thread the second long sleeve on to the wire and fix the swivel using a crimp.

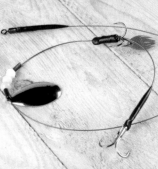

08 The finished rig is given extra attraction by adding a bait flag, once the bait is attached.

In awe of the
sergeant major!

John Bailey recalls a life in love with perch.

I've always been obsessed with perch. The affair began as a six-year-old when I was catching a string of two-pounders from a northern mill reservoir. The fish were so big that they prompted me to buy my first set of scales – some Little Samsons, the then famous spring-balance that measured 4lb in 1oz divisions. My first two-pounder, accurately weighed, pulled the Samsons down a mere 5oz. The following perch, nearly as big, only recorded a measly 4oz.

The Samsons were obviously defective and it was only when I checked them on my mother's full 2lb bag of sugar that I realised it was my own juvenile estimations to blame. After many tears, I realised I had to do better and by the age of eight, I was catching perch that even the Little Samsons agreed were 2lb and over.

Half a century later, the species has seen me catch some whoppers. God knows how many 'twos' and 'threes' I've had but I'm not sure if I've ever caught a UK 'four'. I've enjoyed plenty of this size and above abroad, though – especially on the rivers Volga and Ural.

Believe me, that's where you've got to go if you want an absolute monster. I remember a guide once telling me this: "One kilo, no problem," he said. "Two kilos, very little problem. Three kilos, a bit of a problem. Four kilos, problem. Five kilos, serious problem." Again, believe it or not, I've actually seen a very bad, very blurred photograph of a perch weighing a purported 15lb. Even though the image was bad, the perch is pretty unmistakable.

What I've learnt about perch is this: you can easily have perch in your local water – big perch that is – and not even suspect that they are there. They don't always hunt on the surface and flaunt themselves in a real giveaway fashion. They can be as cunning as a fox. It's no good fishing generally for anything that comes along and expecting a perch to oblige. No, if you want perch, you've got to set out your stall and work for them.

Little deadbaits are great. I spend hours on the waterside and every time I find a small dead fish in the margins, I scoop it up and freeze it. I fish them on the bottom, close to snags. Or with a float, drifting mid-water, searching for a hunting perch pack.

Perch also love worms. Lobs are best. I'll chop up a bunch and throw them in under the trees, next to the reeds. And follow with a half lob freelined on a size eight, allowing the lob to drift down to lie wriggling, irresistible on the bottom.

If all that fails, I'll attack with maggots, feeding heavily and constantly, close to snags. I won't mind if I catch roachlings. Sooner or later, if there are big perch present, they'll make mistakes. I fish light. A 3lb bottom and a 16 hook with two or three maggots impaled. And as soon as I hit a perch, I haul it away from the snags before the fish knows it's hooked.

I'm associated with roach, barbel and chub. But deep down, at heart, I'm always the boy with the Little Samsons. And always waiting to see them pulled down to the fabled 4lb mark by a true UK monster.

Plastics & jellies

It's a modern world, so we'd better look at a selection of new-world lures, including lead-loaded rubber imitations and soft, plastic grubs.

Mann's Hard Nose Jelly

Loaded with salt that helps in fish attraction, these small jelly grubs with curled tails require a large hook to allow the angler to fish them shallow using a simple retrieve. To sink the lure deeper, add a split shot on the line above the hook eye. This allows the jelly to be fished using the sink-and-draw method – and the tail will wiggle like mad!

Berkley Gulp Shaky Shad (smelt)

These soft, plastic lures are impregnated with scents and flavours. They have been a great success in the United States and are now available in the UK. Unweighted, they need a big, heavy, wide-gape hook to make them sink, but as you draw the fish-like lures through the water, not only do they resemble like the real thing but they give off a flavour trail to entice predators to strike.

Daiwa Sonic Shad

This classic shad design has a single, large hook protruding from its back. This allows the angler to slowly work the lure along the bottom of a venue without it snagging on weeds or detritus, making it look like a small fish feeding.

Interex Maxi-Flex Sand Eel

Jig fishing is far more popular in the United States than in the UK, but the eel-like action of these lures when fished using either a sink-and-draw method or jerking tactic can result in explosive takes from pike, zander and perch.

Storm Thundercore Squirter

This little beauty has been described as "brilliant" by the tcf editor. Its downward pointing vein tells you immediately that it's for shallow-water work. It has a thin rubber tail that wobbles as you retrieve, and to add to its predator pulling power it rattles as it moves.

Storm Wildeye Freshwater

These mini freshwater species imitations are designed to be fished using a sink-and-draw-style retrieve. They are armed with a large treble that sits below the internal lead weight and a big single hook that sits well above the top. The shape of their tails add to the lifelike action as the lures travel through the water.

Storm Kicking Segmented Minnow

One for shallower water, this has a downward-pointing vane that draws it upward on the retrieve. The lightly weighted lure has a very thin body with a segmented rear section that imitates the actions of a swimming fish while the holographic internal mesh adds a silver, fish-like glint as it moves.

Deep-pool predators

Fancy bagging a powerful river predator on a lure? Follow **Myles Gascoyne's** advice and you could be in line for a bankside battle.

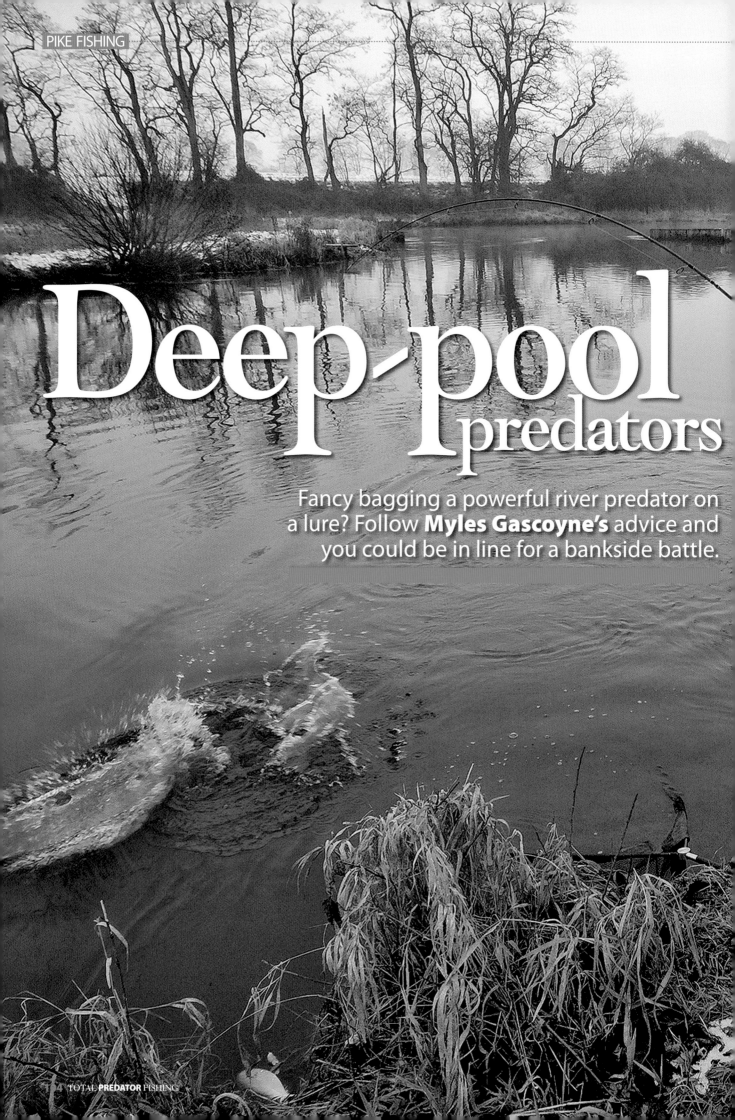

Myles Gascoyne

Hometown: Winchester
Sponsors: Shimano, Rapala, Dynamite Baits and Korda
Personal-best pike: 26lb 2oz

Even on the most challenging days, success can come by exploring every deep pool and marginal bay.

L ure fishing is a great tactic to target pike on stillwaters, but if you want to double the excitement, there's nothing to beat the fight from a double-figure predator on a fast-flowing river. To discover more about how you tackle what to some might be a daunting challenge, we joined one of the south's top lure anglers, Hampshire-based Myles Gascoyne, on a river close to home for some advice on the basics.

The right location

Over winter the many sub-surface features like weed beds and sunken debris disappear, as cold weather and floods kill off the weed and wash it and the rubbish away. With all this cover gone, the baitfish – roach and dace particularly – have to locate permanent cover for safety, so deep river margins and the drop-off of deep pools are a popular choice. A telltale sign that the fish are there would be feeding grebes, small fish popping on the surface and swirls, as pike and perch strike.

This then is the river pike angler's first stop when it comes to swim choice. The problem is how do you know where the features are? Myles suggests there are two ways to do this. The first is to find the holes and deep-water glides during the summer by plumbing up during float fishing sessions. The second is to walk the bank with a set of polarising sunglasses when the water is gin-clear, before the winter floods, to visibly locate possible swims. Either way, by locating these areas in advance you give yourself more fishing time during the short days, rather than wasting time in fishless swims.

The right rod

There is a plethora of lure rods to choose from – all have a place in the predator angler's armoury, but if you are looking for just one rod to cover an occasional trip out, Myles recommends that you look for an 8ft to 8ft 6in rod. However, you also have to look at the casting-weight rating of the rod. For his river fishing, Myles uses a rod that's rated between 10g to 30g with a top section that's soft enough to let him impart life to a small jelly-type lure but, at the same time, is strong enough to allow him to cast and fish 7in baits. The softer-tipped rod is also crucial when using braided main line, as it helps avoid hook-pulls on the strike. With a stiff rod there is more chance of a hook-pull, as there is no stretch with braid and if you strike too hard, the force could rip the lure out of the fish. The softer tip acts as a buffer, so, when the hook sets, the rod compensates for the lack of stretch in the line.

Braid advice

For most of his lure fishing Myles fishes with 30lb braid on a fixed-spool reel. The low diameter of the braid allows his lures to sink without too much drag from the river's fast pace, which could pull the lure off line. He could use a lighter breaking strain line, but one of the hazards of lure fishing is the problem of snags, above and below the water. Lures aren't cheap, so if he is unfortunate enough to get snagged, the strong line allows Myles to pull at the lure with plenty of force to free it. In theory, the hook will come away or it will bend out and the lure pull free. It's then just a matter of replacing the hook and starting again. Myles does have some really expensive lures from America, and if he uses those he'll fish with 65lb braid to ensure he can pull free from any snag. But he believes it's best to avoid them in the first place!

The stronger braid is best fished using a baitcaster reel, as it is possible to damage a fixed-spool reel if you put a lot of pulling pressure on the spool.

Tough trace

If you've ever looked into a pike's mouth, you will know about the vast numbers of needle-sharp teeth it has. These can rip mono to shreds in a matter of moments, so you need to fish with a wire trace. You can make these yourself, but shop-bought ones are pretty cheap. However, Myles believes that the problem with basic wire traces is that often after you catch a fish it becomes badly kinked and is useless to continue with. He recommends that you go the extra mile and buy a few Titanium traces. These are more expensive, but they pay their way over time, as they are very flexible and rarely kink. A 65lb trace will last for some time before you need to replace it.

Pike will seek the cover of deep-water margins, so tread with stealth and explore the water close to the edge.

Hook care

01 Keep a set of long-nosed pliers and a small file on hand for hook maintenance.

02 To make unhooking easier, Myles crushes all the barbs on his hooks.

03 You need really sharp hooks, so if they feel blunt, re-sharpen them with a file.

Myles' top lure choices

01 Favourite soft-plastic lures are (l to r) Curl Tail Shad, Zoota lure & Kickin' Minnow.

02 Favourite hard lures are (l to r) Dive to 20, Musky Mania Jake & Red Head Super Shad Rap.

03 Bright patterns in coloured water and light baits when it's clear? Myles says think again!

So many choices

There are hundreds – if not thousands – of different shaped, size and coloured lures to choose from. Some are made from hard plastic, some soft plastic and some of the really expensive ones are even made from wood. It's easy to get very confused, so Myles has a small selection that he knows will cover the three main tactics he fishes on rivers. As he is looking for fish lurking in the final foot or so of water, his first choice is a shad-patterned soft lure, which he fishes right along the bottom. Next he picks a vaned plastic lure that he cranks to make it swim down, but drifts up when he stops winding. His final pick is a slow-sinking model, which is allowed to sink to a certain depth and retrieved.

Second up is the Storm Kickin' Minnow – this is a slow-sinking lure with a great life-like action. With its underslung, twin sets of trebles, it's best that you do not fish this lure too close to the bottom to avoid catching dead roots and the like.

The last is a hard plastic crank bait, the Rapala DT Sureset, which dives and rises as you wind in and stop retrieving. This is the lure to use in really deep holes.

Myles also has a few variations on these patterns to give him some extra options during the day. A quick look in his box reveals about a dozen or so lures. Being constantly on the move, he only carries his selection in a small purpose-made shoulder bag.

> It takes about five minutes to land, but the 16lb, beautifully marked pike is worth the wait.

Understanding lures

Although some lures give you an idea of what they do on the packaging, Myles suggests that the best way to understand how a lure travels through the water is to find a clear-water venue with a fairly deep margin. You can then watch each lure in turn to see how fast it will sink and how it reacts as you retrieve it – fast and slow.

Colour and pattern can be important. It is said that a bright lure works best in coloured water and a light, shiny one in clear conditions. Myles believes that this is often the case, but some of his best catches have come when he fishes a light-coloured bait in murky water, as it looks more natural – so don't be afraid to go against the grain.

First choice

To keep things simple, Myles selects three patterns for his session. The first is a Storm Wildeye Pro Curl Tail – a jerk-style lure that's fished along and just off the riverbed. With its upper protruding, single hook you are less likely to catch the bottom as you retrieve.

Be sharp

Pike's mouths are extremely bony, so the hooks need to be extra sharp to penetrate on the strike. Out of the packet, the hooks supplied with the lures might feel pretty sharp, but Myles recommends you file them before you start. Before doing so, he crushes the barbs, as it makes it easier to remove the lure. To file the hooks Myles uses a small file and files each at 45 degrees against the point, towards the bend to make each really sharp.

The retrieve

How you retrieve each type of lure is important. To fish productively you firstly need to ensure it doesn't tangle on the cast. Myles believes you need to feather the line on the cast, so the lure lands beyond the swivel of the trace. Once in the water, follow the lure down, and when you reach the desired depth, start the retrieve.

The Curl Tail Shad is fished on the bottom, and once there Myles slowly winds in, twitching the rod top up and down to impart movement, lifting the lure up and letting it drop back. The Kickin'

Tackle talk

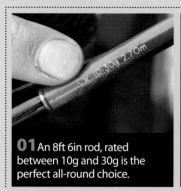

01 An 8ft 6in rod, rated between 10g and 30g is the perfect all-round choice.

02 A fixed-spool reel loaded with 30lb braid is fine for most types of lures.

03 When using big, expensive lures Myles uses 65lb braid on a baitcaster.

04 They cost a bit more, but Titanium traces don't kink, so they last a lot longer.

Myles' top tip

Keep the number of lures you need for the day to a minimum. Take a few different patterns of the same bait, keeping them in a small shoulder bag for ease of transport.

Minnow is fished at any depth and once at the desired depth, the lure is slowly retrieved to make it swim with an enticing, natural-looking action.

Being a crankbait, the DT Sureset is fished on a fast retrieve to make it sink quickly to the desired depth. It has to be retrieved fast, so it's a busy lure to fish, needing plenty of casts to cover all the water.

Myles says it is important to ensure the fish sees the lure, so the retrieve must be at the right pace to make it act naturally enough to interest the pike.

So close

There has been another dumping of snow overnight, so when we arrive at the river the temperature is just above freezing. Will the pike feed? Myles is quietly confident that he will get a take. Being familiar with the stretch of river, Myles starts at a deep pool below a small mid-river island. He starts with the Kickin' Minnow, casting it to the head of the pool and works it back towards him. Myles explores the whole pool without a follow before he switches to the Curl Tail

Shad lure. He works this along the top edge of the pool and on the fifth cast he has a small fish follow. However, the fish shies away, and a further attempt to encourage it to strike fails.

After 20 minutes in the first swim Myles moves on. He reckons that you need no more than 20 casts in any swim to see whether a fish is interested.

A lunker lured

During the day Myles covers about two miles of river, exploring all the obvious marks, including a deep bay close to the bank, but the pike show no interest, except in one pool. Having pricked a fish an hour earlier, he feels it will be worth returning to try again. He tries five or six patterns, but to no avail. A shoal of roach reside in the area, so aware that pike are present and might be tempted, Myles heads upstream, casting a Curl Tail Shad back across at 20-yard intervals.

On the third stop his rod suddenly bends over. The powerful fish raises the temperature as it fights against Myles and the current. It takes about five minutes to land, but the 16lb, beautifully marked pike is worth the wait.

Myles believes it was lying in wait for one of the resident silver fish, so it was fooled by his light-coloured lure.

It was a challenging day, but by exploring the pools and shelves Myles was able to get a result on what to many could seem like a featureless venue.

This cracking, well-conditioned 16lb pike that fell to a slowly worked Curl Tail Shad lure.

Whatever type of lure fishing you enjoy, and whatever lure you're after, The Lure Shed is the only place to visit!

Lures

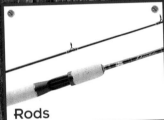
Rods

Reels

Clothing

CRANKBAITS/DIVING LURES

Maxximus Shiner - 7.5cm - 11.5g
A great plug for larger fish such as pike, salmon and bass. Available in 10 superb colour patterns. £9.95

Maxximus JB - 8cm - 8.1g
Suitable for perch, pike, zander, salmon and bass. Available in 10 superb colour patterns. £9.95

Maxximus Crank - 5cm - 7.5g
A smaller plugbait with a quick, darting movement. Perfect for perch, trout, zander and bass. Available in 10 superb colour patterns. £9.95

Conrad Pike Beast - 17.5cm - 55g
The ultimate floating pike bait with irresistible action, available in a range of 12 excellent colours. £6.35

Conrad Big Dive - 17cm - 80g
A large and very effective deep-diving lure for those big predatory fish. Available in 7 great colour patterns. £6.95

Eco Snake - 12cm - 18g
A multi-jointed shallow-diving lure with incredible action. Available in 5 great colours. £3.95

Eco Jointed Fat - 8cm - 14g
A deep-bodied crankbait with two segments to provide a superb action. Available in 4 great colours. £3.95

SOFTBAITS

SoftFish Vertical Jig - 8.5cm - 11g
A big favourite with all anglers. £1.95

Conrad Tail Crawler
The ultimate softbait. Irresistible to pike and other predatory fish. Available in 2 sizes and a fantastic range of colours.
20cm - 45g - £4.95
30cm - 115g - £6.35

Conrad Great SoftFish - 15cm - 65g
Its movement and vibration in the water is guaranteed to attract predatory fish. These large softbaits come in 5 great colours. £5.95

MICRO PLUGBAITS

Maxximus Minnow - 3cm - 1.1g
A micro floating plugbait with lots of movement and vibration. Designed for perch and trout. Available in 7 superb colour patterns. £9.95

Maxximus Shad - 4cm - 2.7g
This lure has an awesome amount of wobble, roll and movement. Ideal for trout, perch and zander. Available in 10 superb colour patterns. £9.95

JERKBAITS

Conrad Melvin Jerk
A very effective slow-sinking jerkbait. Available in 2 sizes and a fantastic range of colours.
11cm - 43g - £4.45
13cm - 60g - £4.95

Maxximus Fantasy Jerk - 13cm - 85g
A superb deep-bodied sinking jerkbait. Available in 6 great colour patterns. £9.25

SURFACE LURES

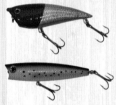

Eco Popper - 6.5cm - 6g
A classic surface popper lure in 4 great colours. £2.95

Conrad Popper
A top-quality, time-tested surface lure for pike, bass and other predatory fish. Available in 2 sizes and a fantastic range of colours.
8cm - 12g - £3.95
11cm - 19g - £4.25

SWIMBAITS

Conrad ActionPlay
A range of multi-movement plugs to drive fish wild. Available in 2 sizes and 3 fantastic colours.
15cm - 41g - £11.95
20cm - 83g - £14.95

SPOONS

Tiger Singo Spoon - 26g. Awesome lures with an amazing finish and in 7 great colours. £3.75

SPINNERS

Finest quality fishing spinners by ILBA of Italy. A huge range of single and tandem patterns from 2g to 36g in various colours. Perfect for all predators. Prices from just £1.45

SPINNERBAITS

Finest quality spinnerbait lures by ILBA of Italy in 10 great colour patterns.
19g - £6.35

All of these products and more available at
www.lureshed.co.uk
Tel: 01425 688212

Innovation in predator fishing is limited, but **Mick Brown's** kebab rig has taken fishing deadbaits to the next level, especially when popped up over weed!

A taste for kebabs

When I came up with the idea for the kebab rig a couple of years ago, it received quite a mixed reception from the country's pike anglers. I regularly follow the comments from the pike fishing forums, those I pick up at meetings and on the bank, and it's interesting that they usually fall into two camps. Some pike anglers are totally in favour of the kebab system, having used the technique correctly and reaped the benefits, while others dismiss it out of hand. They don't see how it can be used to make pike fishing better for them or for the pike. Radical ideas often take a while to catch on, and the kebab is certainly a very different approach to catching pike compared to other deadbaiting methods. What I don't want to do is try and ram my philosophy down other anglers' throats. I would rather try and guide them into discovering what I have for themselves.

A safer way
Some anglers don't understand why I use this method. First of all I should explain that it isn't a revolutionary bagging-up method. There ARE times when the kebab does outfish normal deadbait tactics,

Mick Brown
Hometown: Market Deeping, Lincs
Sponsors: Dynamite Baits, Rapala and Shimano

but my main concern is the safety of the angler and the pike. As I see it, a method that involves using just one hook, which simplifies netting without tangling and makes for easy handling and unhooking, has got to be better. It may have a few flaws, but I remain confident that when using this rig, overall my fishing feels safer, relatively trouble free and the pike get a better deal with more efficient handling.

These benefits are enough for me, but there is also the bonus of the fantastic scent trail, which exudes from a properly prepared bait. I'm sure that this is instrumental in helping pike and other predators to find the baits more quickly, especially in weedy waters.

I really believe in this approach, so it's time to get off my soapbox and recount our recent day on the bank…

The right venue

I arrived at dawn at a lake, which I would describe as a 'runs' water. It's the ideal place to use kebabs because of the amount of fish handling that's likely. Would I use the kebab on a hard water where the fish are bigger and I might only get one run in the session? Yes, I would, if it was appropriate to that water.

If the water demanded bigger deadbaits, livebaits or lures, then I would choose the most likely method to get a result. In prebaiting situations, though, and on hard-fished waters, yes I would use kebabs for bigger fish and I have caught several twenties in doing so.

For this session on the 60-acre lake, the likelihood of catching pike was good, as the bay I fished was full of roach. Even as I arrived I saw fish scatter over the surface as the pike attacked the shoals from time to time.

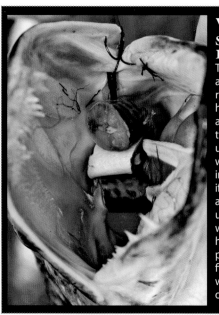

Why use single treble rigs?

There are a number of advantages to using rigs with a single treble hook. The first is you avoid getting flying trebles – that is an un-baited set of hooks which could end up in the angler's hand if the pike thrashes about when it's being unhooked. Secondly, with only one set of hooks to remove, the process is quicker, so the fish is returned to the water with a minimum of fuss and stress.

The pike were on a feeding frenzy, striking at silver-fish shoals all day, but it didn't stop them from taking Mick's baits.

Mick's packet baits

01 Dynamite Baits' ready-made pop-up kebabs are ideal for fishing on weedy-bottomed lakes.

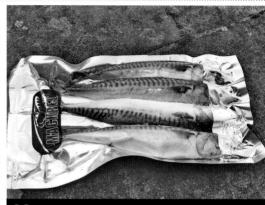

02 To make your own kebabs, make sure you get hold of slim-profile baits like joey mackerel.

Conventional rigs

I needed to get a feel for the swim, so before casting the first kebab, I started with a conventional float-fished deadbait. Nothing happened for about 30 minutes and after retrieving the baits I found that they were stuck in dense bottom weed. My next ploy was to fish a suspended half herring deadbait above the weed. This is something I often do on weedy-bottom venues. It works fine, but it's not so easy to be sure how far you are off bottom in swims where the depth varies. They are also prone to drifting away in unfavourable winds. This happened a few times where the bait eventually drifted into weed, and although I did get a few runs I only connected with and landed one fish.

> This was one of those special days when runs came with the regularity we all dream about.

I felt it was one of those days where the pike would favour a smaller offering and it was the right time to put out a kebab rig. I reckoned a float-fished pop-up version to get it just above the weed was the best tactic.

Popped-up option

With quick-change links on my line, it was a simple task to change to the traces, which I had already baited with kebabs. I used Dynamite kebab baits straight from the bag. These were mounted on a one-treble trace with a size 4 treble. This is the ideal size for efficient hooking.

Before casting, I checked the presentation in the clear-water margin. It stood out brilliantly above the weed with the bright red polyball boldly giving away its presence. I was happy with

the rigs, so two rods were cast out, both with kebabs attached. I felt sure we would catch, as the conditions were perfect. Only the day before I had bagged up on a different water, so I was buzzing with confidence.

Instant action

A run came pretty quick on the right-hand rod, and as I guided the pike to the landing net, the left-hand bait was taken! Now here is another instance of where using one hook is beneficial. With no flying treble to snag in the net I was able to land the second pike without a hitch.

It was then very easy to lift the net without fear of the two pike spinning round and snagging the trebles. It was also easy to remove them both from the mesh and onto the unhooking mat. Both trebles were easily visible and simply removed. There was none of that fiddling around for ages with two hooks where there's a much greater danger of damaging both your fingers and the pike. So after a quick pose for the camera, they were back in the water in no time at all.

Plenty of spares

In preparation, I had already mounted further kebab baits on spare traces and they were clipped on and back out as quickly as possible. I'd kept the weight used to counteract the buoyancy in the rig to a minimum. Only 12g was needed. This allowed the baits to sit gently on the bottom weed covering. Ten minutes later, I was away again and another pike was netted, unhooked and returned with the minimum of fuss and risk.

The right setup

As with any method, deep hooking can occur if you don't set the float correctly and don't strike straightaway. The float needs to be set only very slightly overdepth to give sensitive bite indication. The depth in my swim was about six feet deep, so I set my rig overdepth by about a foot.

Striking has to be instant, as with any pike method, to ensure the fish doesn't take the bait too far into its mouth. I have the confidence to strike kebab runs straightaway. With a large treble and a relatively small bait, there is no reason to do otherwise. In mild weather this is particularly important when the pike are likely to bolt down any bait. It's then that I switch to using semi-barbed trebles.

A dream day

This was to prove to be one of those special days when runs came with the regularity we all dream about. I'm not kidding myself that other methods wouldn't have caught, but I really enjoyed the session because with my single-treble-hook tactic, handling the fish was so simple. It really minimises the chance of getting a hook in the hand from a flying treble and there's less chance of getting snagged up in the net. More importantly, one set of hooks made it easier and quicker to remove from the fish's jaws. This enabled all the fish to be returned with little fuss and the minimum of stress.

Double's delight

Over the next few hours I added plenty more pike to my tally including a few quality doubles, all in pristine condition with superb markings. It had been an excellent day's pike fishing in the conditions in which they had been caught.

As the day wore on, though, the sun got brighter, the pike fed less and less in the gin-clear water and the sport petered out.

Please give the kebab a try before you dismiss its benefits. If you have any doubts, try it on one rod and see how handling compares with other rigs. Use it on waters where pike readily take deadbaits, and especially on 'bag-up' waters where you have a lot of handling to do.

Not just pike

It has also worked for other species and in particular catfish. I've had a lot of zander, a few chub and, surprisingly, quite a few carp, especially on lamprey-baited kebabs, too. Keeping an open mind with all your fishing is the way forward, I'm sure. Kebabs are now an everyday part of my pike fishing repertoire and I get reports all the time from anglers who have tried kebab fishing and changed their fishing for the better.

Mick Brown's feeding tip

Mick uses his kebabs on traces with single treble hooks. To ensure his bait is back in the water soon after catching, he makes up plenty of ready-baited traces in advance.

All the pike Mick caught were wonderfully marked.